Travels with a Primate

Travels with a Primate

Around the world with Archbishop Robert Runcie

TERRY WAITE

HarperCollins*Publishers*

HarperCollins*Publishers*
77–85 Fulham Palace Road, London W6 8JB
www.**fireandwater**.com

First published in Great Britain in 2000 by HarperCollins*Publishers*
This edition 2001

3 5 7 9 10 8 6 4 2

Illustrations by Josephine Blake (Beehive Illustration)

Chapters 3 and 6 have previously appeared in a
slightly different form in *Travellers' Tales*,
written by members of The Travellers Club

Terry Waite asserts the moral right to be
identified as the author of this work

A catalogue record for this book is
available from the British Library

ISBN 0 00 710633 5

Printed and bound in Great Britain by
Clays Ltd, St Ives plc

Dedicated with affection to

Dr Robert Runcie

Archbishop of Canterbury 1980–91

and to

Richard and John

Chaplains and travelling companions

Contents

Acknowledgements

First of all, sincere thanks to Robert Runcie, Richard Chartres, John Witheridge and Sam Van Culin for their willingness to allow me to write this light-hearted account of some of our travels together.

My old friend John Curtis read the manuscript in an early draft and as always was more than helpful with constructive criticism. Peter Drew and James Newcome also gave invaluable support.

My agent, Mark Lucas, was surprised to receive a different book from the one he originally expected, but dealt with the situation with his usual skill and good nature. Sarah Douglas-Pennant typed the script from her home in rural Suffolk and Frances, my wife, carefully read the proofs. Rory and Kristine gave me hospitality in Cape Town while I wrote Chapter 12 and Mafuta and Agnes shared their silent company with me at the foot of Table Mountain.

I struggled for a long time to find an appropriate title for the book and eventually Chris, my neighbour in London, came up with one that could not be bettered. I only wish I had had the wit to think of it.

Finally, my editor James Catford remained consistently supportive and cheerful and I owe him my gratitude.

I am greatly indebted to all the above, but of course accept total responsibility for what is written. It has been fun to remember and write about some happy days spent in the company of good and loyal friends.

Introduction

Just a few days before he died I spoke with Robert Runcie on the telephone. It was our normal practice to phone each other every week or so. He had recently returned to his home in St Albans after taking a short cruise which he suspected would be his last.

Several months earlier I had sent him a draft of this manuscript. He laughed as he recalled the two fund-raising evenings we had conducted for Emmaus, a charity for the homeless, when we both spoke about the lighter side of life at Lambeth. Some material from those evenings eventually found its way into this book.

'No one,' he said, 'ought to occupy a position of responsibility unless they have a sense of humour.' He then gave me a mischievous quote for the cover: 'I was determined to stay alive until this book was published.' He asked me when that would be.

'October the 2nd,' I answered.

'Good heavens,' he exclaimed, 'that's my birthday.'

For my part this was a happy coincidence, but we agreed there and then that we would do something special on that day.

Alas, that was not to be. Robert died peacefully on 11 July 2000 after a long and courageous battle with ill health. Although he did not live to see the publication of *Travels*, he read it and was able to correct one or two matters of detail. We failed to agree as to whether it was the band of the Grenadier or Scots Guards that played at the Lambeth Palace Garden Party (Chapter 15). He insisted that it was the Scots Guards, and who am I to argue?

His funeral service was conducted in the Abbey at St Albans on 22 July 2000, and was a wonderful celebration of his life. His friends had gathered from across the world and the many who could not gain admittance stood outside the building which he loved so much.

Although he always claimed he was not musical, he chose the music for the service and it was splendid. Afterwards, the immediate members of his family left the church for the burial while the remainder of the congregation sat in silence. Then we heard the haunting strain of bagpipes. Outside, a piper was playing 'Dr Robert Runcie, MC' as a final tribute. I remembered his joke about this composition (Chapter 17) and smiled to myself. I said a small prayer of gratitude for the life of a good and brave man, then stood and walked out into the warm July sunshine.

'You know,' someone said as we stood chatting afterwards, 'he inspired me to live a better life.' Yes, I thought, he must have encouraged and inspired thousands similarly during his lifetime.

This light-hearted volume of anecdotes is but a partial account of some of the events we shared across the world during our time together. Not only did he inspire me, he also gave me many happy and amusing memories. I dedicate it with affection to him, and to my former colleagues, the chaplains who served him so well.

Terry Waite CBE
July 2000

1

The Rainmaker

In 1486, when Cardinal Morton travelled from Lambeth to Canterbury to be what was then known as 'enthronized' as Lord Cardinal Archbishop, he was on the road for six days. His first stop was at Croydon, where there was a fine old palace. Duly fortified, he drove onwards to Knole. The next night saw him in Maidstone, following which he stopped over at Charing. On Saturday night he was in Chartham and on Sunday morning he made a grand entry into Canterbury itself. Even present-day commuters will have to agree that matters have improved slightly since then.

In those days Archbishops travelled with a goodly number of companions. On his trip to Canterbury it is said that

Morton was 'greatly accompanied'. The famed Becket made his entry with some 200 knights, each of whom was accompanied by a squire and a body of able retainers. Even Archbishop Whitgift, who was noted for his humility and lack of display, travelled with some 200 attendants and at least 800 horsemen. It is all pretty impressive stuff and makes the archiepiscopal journeys of today look not just parsimonious but positively mean. On his domestic travels throughout the British Isles, Archbishop Runcie, who took possession of the throne of Augustine in 1980, would travel with his driver and his Chaplain. On his overseas journeys throughout the Anglican Communion I would also accompany him. It was a far cry from the good old days.

Robert Runcie enjoyed travelling. His mother worked for a time as a hairdresser on the Cunard line and frequently journeyed to and from New York. I do not believe that she took the fledgling Archbishop along with her, but it could be that he inherited his love of travel from her.

He travelled throughout Europe during World War II, when he served with distinction in the Scots Guards, and also later, when he made frequent visits to the Orthodox Church. He had visited the United States occasionally, but Africa and most of Asia was unknown to him. That was one of the reasons why he employed me. I had spent a good deal of my life travelling throughout the world and had gained a reasonable knowledge of the workings of the Church in far-flung regions. The Chaplain was thoroughly conversant with matters ecclesiastical, but also had a limited knowledge of the world beyond Europe. So, when social, political or ecclesiastical briefings

2

were required on Nigeria, Burma or some equally distant territory, it was to yours truly that the Archbishop turned.

Although in later years I was dubbed by the press as 'the Archbishop's envoy', my correct title was in fact 'the Archbishop's Advisor on Anglican Communion Affairs'. Clearly this had rather a pompous ring about it and was far too long for any newspaper to print, and so the term 'envoy' stuck. My office was situated in Lambeth Palace, the official London residence of the Archbishop. The Chaplain was also based there, along with other members of the Archbishop's modest *familia*.

Much of the history of the Palace was only vaguely known to me on the morning in 1979 when I walked from Waterloo Station to begin my first day in the service of the one-hundred-and-second Archbishop of Canterbury. Although Robert Runcie had been nominated to the office of Archbishop, he had yet to be enthroned in his cathedral in Canterbury. His first task was to establish himself in Lambeth.

I approached the massive main wooden doors of the Palace. They were firmly closed, as was the smaller side door intended for those entering on foot. Beside the door was an ancient bell pull and I gave it a hefty tug. Somewhere behind the walls there was a faint ringing sound. I waited and after a suitable interval gave the handle another pull. A passage from the Koran came to mind, in which it says that those who mock the beliefs of others will approach the door of paradise only to have it firmly shut in their face. They will then move to another door, and another, and this unhappy state of affairs will continue throughout eternity. Fortunately, as this was Lambeth in South London and not Elysium, that was not to be my fate just yet. After the third yank on the bell, a key turned in the lock and the door slowly opened inwards, revealing an elderly man who smiled and welcomed me across the threshold.

'I'm sorry to keep you waiting,' he said. 'It's the telephone, you see. They ring me about everything and what with their questions, opening the gates, sorting the mail, dealing with the newspapers and trying to get a bit of breakfast, it's all a bit of a rush.'

It transpired that the gatekeeper not only had his modest office in The Great Gateway but actually lived there also. Subsequently I learned that there was a substantial gateway at Lambeth as long ago as 1321. After the destructive wars between the houses of York and Lancaster, Cardinal Archbishop Morton (known as 'the building Archbishop') set to work and Morton's Tower stands at the entrance to the Palace to this very day, now the home of the Lambeth gatekeeper. Some time later I discovered that Cardinal Morton also had his sitting room and bedroom in the Western Tower of the gateway. His audience chamber was situated directly over the main wooden doors, and nearby there was a small prison for the detention of heretics and disaffected noblemen. During my time at Lambeth this room was vacant – although it was not difficult to think of suitable tenants.

My first weeks in the Palace were somewhat chaotic. The Archbishop had brought with him his personal Chaplain and his private secretary, but had inherited most of his other personal staff from his predecessor. Much time was spent sorting out the basic administration on the ground and first floors and the Archbishop's wife laboured long and hard to get their living quarters in the upper regions to her liking. Eventually, some semblance of order was established and I moved into my office overlooking the main courtyard. It was a pleasant room and old plans showed that the wing in which it was situated had been added in the early 1800s. In those days, my study was the Chaplain's room, the Archbishop's secretary lodged next door and the Archbishop's library and private sitting room were at the other end overlooking the garden. Not much had changed since then, except that the Archbishop and the Chaplain had moved a little further along the main corridor.

Once we were installed, it was time to get down to some real work.

Just across the River Thames in prosperous Westminster there is a less ancient building which housed the Anglican Consultative Council. The Council was a relatively new body and was charged with co-ordinating the work of the Anglican Communion throughout the world. There was a time when the whole of Westminster was a happy and profitable stamping ground for the C of E, but in recent years the Church has disposed of much of the family silver by selling off many of the properties it owned or leased. Today the office of the Council is situated in the Waterloo Road. In my day, however, the Secretary General resided in Westminster.

The Revd Sam Van Culin, who occupied this important role, was an amiable American whom I had known for very many years. Our paths first crossed when, as a young man, I went to work for the Church in Uganda. He was then based in New York and was responsible for the overseas activities of the

American Episcopal Church. As in those days the American Church paid my salary, he ensured that I received my monthly cheque. He was a man of unfailing good humour, diplomacy and patience and his knowledge of the Anglican Communion was unrivalled.

From time to time, the Revd Sam would leave Westminster, stroll gently across Lambeth Bridge, wait for a time while the gatekeeper dealt with the telephone, cross the courtyard and ascend the main staircase leading to the Archbishop's study.

'Your Grace,' he remarked on one of his quarterly visits to the Palace in the early eighties, 'Nigeria is one of the fastest growing parts of the Anglican Communion.'

The Archbishop was gratified. Hardly a week passed by without the British press detailing the imminent demise of the Church of England, so to hear news of actual growth was cheering.

'I would suggest, Your Grace, that when it could be arranged you might consider visiting West Africa. Nigeria is a very large country and you won't be able to travel everywhere, but you would receive an extremely warm welcome.'

This suggestion appealed to the Archbishop because, around the time of the Revd Sam's visit, the Prime Minister, Margaret Thatcher, had taken to using the Archbishop's residence for target practice. This was nothing new, of course. In the days when Archbishops also held high State office, they frequently found themselves in the midst of political intrigue – so much so that they retained a substantial body of men-at-arms and lodged them in the Guard Chamber, strategically placed between the main gate and the private apartments. To this day there is a Guard Room at Lambeth, although the suits of armour, muskets and bandoleers disappeared many years ago.

It is said that the wrath of the PM had been incurred because Dr Runcie had been unwise enough to preach about reconciliation and forgiveness following the Falklands campaign. I am not suggesting for one moment that, in considering a visit overseas, the Archbishop was considering a retreat. After all, he had won a Military Cross during World War II. However, a visit to encourage African Anglicans, especially as the weather was none too warm in London, had its attractions. The Archbishop also had to discharge his responsibilities overseas. The matter was duly passed to me for attention.

Any individual who has charge of developing a travel programme for a personage of religious or political importance will face problems. Everyone wants to get in on the act. I have exchanged notes, and from time to time co-operated, with those who plan royal and papal visits. The royal planners were very polite – some might say over-polite – but utterly ruthless. The papal planners were just utterly ruthless. I tried to be ruthless, but having been nurtured in the C of E, compromise was an indelible part of my being. One simply did one's best to keep the programme for a visit within manageable proportions.

When a request for a stop to be included in a visit was refused, the supplicant would frequently approach the Archbishop directly. The Archbishop, always ready to please, would invariably smile and inform the individual that the only reason he desired to visit Nigeria was to lay the foundation stone of the Moses Memorial Church, and even though the site could only be approached by walking six miles along a bush track, he would do it before breakfast.

'Just see Mr Waite,' he would say. Mr Waite would then do his best to show the ruthless side of Lambeth and say that it was impossible to visit the building. Following that display of bravado, either Mr Waite made an enemy for life, or some compromise was reached.

The programme for Nigeria was a series of compromises, but on paper it appeared workable. When it was put before the Archbishop's Chaplain, however, he groaned. 'This will kill us all,' he muttered as he examined the draft programme for the West African tour. 'When are we going to get time to write all the sermons needed? What about all these extra speeches? Ye gods, this looks awful!'

I had to agree with him. It looked awful. Add in humidity, heat, indifferent food, tortuous journeys and very long church services, and it promised to be a taxing visit.

The evening before an overseas visit was, quite literally, a nightmare. Not having an army of retainers to call upon, the Chaplain had to take responsibility for ensuring that the ecclesiastical robes and the portable archiepiscopal processional cross were safely packed. I had to ensure that the reams of briefing papers were assembled and ready to slip into the Archbishop's eager hand so that he would be able to step into any gathering during the tour, greet everyone by name and enquire not only about their children but about their grandchildren also. As you might imagine, there were some rather long lists in the Nigerian files.

The Chaplain's study on the evening prior to our departure resembled clearing-out day at a theatrical costumier. The colourful plumage of ecclesiastical disguise lay strewn across the room, whilst behind a massive carved oak desk sat the Chaplain, scribbling for all he was worth with a quill pen. This was his preferred method of writing and he constantly produced elegantly written and legible scripts.

There was no avoiding the huge number of speeches and sermons that needed to be prepared before a visit such as this. In the days when communication throughout Africa was by cleft stick, a visiting dignitary could easily get away with just two or three well-constructed sermons and a speech or two. As the Archbishop sat in his cabin aboard ship, sailing out to Africa and sipping a little white wine to aid the digestion, there was ample time not only to write sermons for the forthcoming tour but also to write a couple of books into the bargain. Since British Airways came into their own, however, there was no longer the opportunity to enjoy such luxury.

The Archbishop's time was increasingly constrained. When he was not occupied protecting the Palace from attacks out of Westminster, he was fully engaged in attempting to comprehend the inscrutable finances of the C of E, or placating some Bishop or other who desired to transfer to Rome, if only he could find some way of dealing with his wife. Inevitably the pressure of life meant that others had to be recruited to do some drafting for the sermons and speeches. Much of this work fell on the Chaplain, who possessed a unique gift in this specialized area, but even he had his limitations. Several weeks before the visit to Nigeria, we had conferred about the problem.

'Look,' he said. 'We've got to spread the load. It's totally impossible to manage all this material. What about that chap from overseas? You remember, the priest who does a bit of journalism.'

I did indeed remember. The priest to whom the Chaplain referred lived in foreign parts and, from what I could gather, edited a magazine that dealt with the more esoteric areas of ritual in worship. He had frequently offered his scribing services and had been robustly rejected. Now, however, his name appeared like a bright light on a barren landscape.

There was no harm in giving him a try, I said, especially as we would be able to go through the material and our diligent and faithful master always put his own unique stamp on any script before delivery. The priest was contacted accordingly. By return mail he promised to deliver bundles of the highest quality scripts within 24 hours. I exaggerate, of course. Perhaps I simply ought to record that he was enthusiastic.

We waited expectantly. Each morning, sackloads of mail arrived from individuals who wished to share their spiritual insights with Lord Runcie. The mail was of unfailing interest to those curious about the bizarre in life. Some correspondents had had visions of impending doom and urged His Grace to ascend into the nearest pulpit and warn the unsuspecting populace that, unless they repented, trouble was in store. Others claimed to have identified the Antichrist and were amazed that Dr Runcie did not share their perception. The Archbishop's long-suffering secretary carefully read each letter and made provision for a polite reply.

Each morning the Chaplain and I anxiously examined the mail for the promised scripts. Alas, there was nothing. Finally, on the eve of departure, a little packet arrived. It was hardly a bundle; in fact it was little more than two or three pages of badly typed script, in which the writer had selected a text and surrounded it with enough platitudes to send the most gospel-hardened Nigerian running for shelter.

The Chaplain, a man of philosophical equanimity, gave a long sigh, handed me the meagre script and continued to write furiously. I placed the document in my inside pocket and resumed my packing of the briefing case.

Morning dawned and the Archbishop appeared. As a former member of the Brigade of Guards, he was accustomed to packing his own personal items and he did so with diligence and skill. Occasionally a purple sock or the sleeve of a jacket became jammed in the case, but this misfortune happens to the best of us and is easily remedied. Unfortunately, more often than not, when His Grace attempted to return the protruding items of personal apparel to their correct place, several others would attempt to escape. This annoyance was frequently a cause of delay, but everyone took it in good humour and his excellent chauffeur John Brown speedily loaded the Archbishop's car. I use the adjective 'excellent' deliberately. Of all the staff at Lambeth Palace, John Brown must be singled out for calmness and competence. Never once did I see him agitated or excited. He would drive the length and breadth of the British Isles with the serenity of a seraphim and was worth at least 500 horsemen.

Unlike his illustrious predecessors from the early part of the century, who took a leisurely drive to Southampton and a short nap before dinner on the boat, Dr Runcie was driven to that hub of mechanical nastiness, Heathrow Airport.

Admittedly the pain was eased considerably by being driven to the Alcock and Brown VIP suite, hidden somewhere within the airport's remoter regions. Press photographers lingered outside the front of the building, snapping away merrily as we arrived.

'I can't understand why every time I come to the airport these men appear,' said the Archbishop.

We did not have the heart to inform him that they took his picture as a precaution against the plane going down. If such an unhappy event were to take place, they could claim to have the last photograph of Dr Runcie before he met his Maker and, I assume, his Employer. Special permission had to be obtained before representatives of the press could enter the lounge. Normally they left us alone at the door of the suite and we were granted a few moments of peace before being driven to the aircraft.

The journey to Lagos was uneventful. The Archbishop read his notes, the Chaplain scribbled and I brought one or two of the briefing papers up to date. There was the customary line-up on arrival, headed by Archbishop Timothy of Nigeria and supported by the great, the good and the indifferent. Timothy was one of the more senior Archbishops in Africa, if not in the whole Communion. He had been born in Nigeria and could be somewhat sharp with his staff. On one occasion when I was visiting him, his unfortunate Chaplain poked his head around the door with an urgent message and was smartly told, 'Get your black, cotton-picking head out of here.' Not the sort of politically correct comment one hears every day from an Archbishop, but it was clear and to the point and the Chaplain disappeared.

Beyond the perimeter fence of the airport, several hundred loyal Anglicans had assembled. They waved, sang and generally did their best to convince Dr Runcie that this was indeed the fastest growing branch of the Anglican Communion. The two Archbishops greeted each other and His Grace was introduced to the cast of characters who had gathered to welcome him.

It was on that very first evening that Dr Runcie demonstrated that he was in possession of worldly wisdom as well as the spiritual variety. A prominent businessman in the capital had arranged for specially invited guests to attend an evening at his house, where His Grace was to be guest of honour. He had prepared a magnificent buffet, consisting of oysters, clams, crabs and other denizens of the deep known only to the inhabitants of African coastal regions.

Dr Runcie, always modest in his eating and drinking habits, examined the spread with the eagle eye of one who had survived countless parochial bun fights and a lifetime of contract catering. 'I think I'll have a little bread and butter,' he said.

Bread and butter were produced and, to cries of 'Are you sure that's enough?' and 'Have a spoonful of this delicious fish pâté, Your Grace', Dr Runcie immersed himself in conversation.

The Chaplain, showing equal restraint, sipped a little Mateus Rosé, quickly put his glass down and was seen to eat or drink nothing further that evening.

Alas, there is always one fool at a party. 'I'd sooner keep Waite a week than a fortnight,' said the Archbishop to a group of Nigerian clergymen who were commenting on my height. 'He can eat, believe me.' The host certainly believed Dr Runcie and urged me to sample a little of everything that was on offer. It tasted good. True, the lobster tail seemed somewhat iffy, but I fondly imagined that liberal quantities of rosé would act as a disinfectant if necessary.

To say that I had a troubled night would be an understatement. I shall go no further. The following morning we were due to journey 100 miles or so in an official convoy, complete with police outriders. I dragged my miserable body to the car immediately behind the Archbishop's vehicle. The Chaplain, already seated, was scribbling as usual. 'Ah,' he beamed, 'from your countenance, it appears that the tropical heat is already having its effect!'

I managed a wan smile and sat beside him. Half a dozen white-jacketed police outriders kicked their motorcycles into life and off we roared. Why it was considered necessary to travel along narrow dirt roads at speeds in excess of 70 miles per hour, I know not. After a mile or so, one of the white jackets attempted a tricky manoeuvre, lost control of his machine and disappeared into the bush.

'Leave him!' shouted the police escort sitting next to our driver. 'We can't stop. We must move on.'

We moved rapidly onwards, while the pains in my inner regions became increasingly acute. The sweat gathered on my brow and I clenched and unclenched my fists furiously. 'We must stop,' I muttered. 'I can't go on like this. Nature isn't just calling, she's bellowing.'

At that point we passed through a village street lined by hundreds of fast-growing, flag-waving Anglicans. 'We can't stop here,' said the policeman. 'The Archbishop would be mobbed.'

We left the village behind and the driver communicated with the lead car on his radio. 'They say we can't stop. We must continue.'

By now I was ready to dive headlong through the side window. 'Stop, for goodness' sake, stop!' I shouted. 'Pull out of the convoy.'

To my relief and surprise, the driver did just that. We were in the middle of a land that resembled the surface of the moon. One or two cactuses were dotted here and there, and that was all. I sprinted out of the car and across the lunar landscape. Never have I felt such relief.

When I returned to the car, we continued our journey and the Chaplain resumed his scribbling. 'By the way,' he said, 'that sermon we commissioned. Might I take a look at it for a moment? There might be one quotation we could use.'

'Sorry,' I replied. 'It's just been put to good use.'

The Chaplain sighed and resumed his drafting. In the car ahead of us Dr Runcie chatted amiably with Archbishop Timothy. At least I had occasion to be grateful to our absent scribe, although I never had the heart to tell him just how useful his script had been.

* * * * *

Although the name of Jane Montgomery Campbell is largely forgotten throughout the land, every year, when churches are stacked with marrows, pumpkins and tins of processed peas, there remain a goodly number of people who sing one of her compositions. I refer, of course, to that old favourite 'We

15

plough the fields and scatter'. The hymn is well known. It relates the story of how good seed planted by diligent country-folk is fed and watered by the Almighty, who sends snow in winter, gentle breezes and sunshine in the summer and soft, refreshing rain in between times. All very satisfactory. However, observant travellers will have noted that the great farmer in the sky tends to be a little forgetful from time to time, with the consequence that certain regions on this planet receive no liquid refreshment for year after year, while rustic planters in other parts of the globe watch helplessly as their turnips disappear under countless gallons of water.

Perhaps I am being unfair to the Almighty. It might be that He is kept so busy attending to crisis management in the Church of England that He is obliged to delegate His agricultural responsibilities to one who is, quite frankly, less than competent. Theologians who happen to stumble across this book will no doubt write to me with the authoritative viewpoint about this unfortunate state of affairs. Meanwhile, the fact is that some in this world suffer shortage and some enjoy plenty.

During his long and exhausting expedition through Nigeria, Dr Runcie – a man who, although born in Liverpool, nevertheless took a deep interest in rural affairs – was able to observe for himself what happens when the tap on the heavenly hosepipe remains in the off position for a dozen years or more.

We were travelling somewhere in the north of Nigeria. Time has dimmed my memory as to the exact location. All I remember is that it was an exceptionally dry part of the country. Dr Runcie, no mean judge of matters agrarian, commented to Archbishop Timothy that the ground appeared to be a trifle parched. Archbishop Timothy did not reply immediately. He was too wise for that. He had spent a lifetime dodging the slings and arrows deployed by the multitude of political and tribal factions that constituted Nigeria, and thus had learned to think before replying. His response, when uttered, was entirely factual. 'There has been no rain for 10 years.'

Dr Runcie's compassionate brow furrowed. Ten years without rain surely went beyond forgetfulness, gross negligence or divine retribution. He was reluctant to consider the latter. Indeed, the more he thought about any of the options, the more puzzled he became. Conscious of the fact that he was conversing with a political survivor of the highest order, Dr Runcie was equally factual in his reply. 'Ten years is a very long time.' Archbishop Timothy remained silent and the two fathers of the Church continued their pilgrimage through the desert.

Our destination on this particular day was, not surprisingly, an Anglican church. Dr Runcie was due to preach and afterwards attend a reception given in his honour. His Grace had attended scores of such functions back in England and was a past master at conversing with all and sundry on a variety of topics. Nevertheless, social events following a service were taxing. 'It's enforced geniality,' he once said to me, 'that wears you out.' As one whose total life consisted of being amiable, I imagined that he would be utterly exhausted much of the time. I was wrong. He possessed the energy of 10 men.

We progressed across the dusty plain until we observed signs indicating that we were about to enter a small town.

There was great excitement within the Anglican community, as some time earlier His Holiness the Pope had paid a state visit to the country and considerably boosted the image of the Roman Catholic Church, while at the same time depleting its fortune. (I refer, of course, to treasure garnered on earth. Heavenly treasure was no doubt increased immeasurably.) Our càr slowed to allow us to pass through a triumphal arch that had been erected across the roadway. A rather sinister-looking picture of Dr Runcie adorned the gateway, but this proved to be only a preliminary indication of what was to come.

The street broadened into a wide boulevard with a thin central reservation. Along this narrow strip, stretching as far as the eye could see, life-size cardboard cut-out images of His Grace of Canterbury had been erected. The image portrayed was of the Archbishop in full ecclesiastical garb, clutching the Canterbury Cross and smiling somewhat cynically. Here was actual proof that the Secretary General of the Anglican Council had not been wrong when he indicated rapid growth in Nigeria. There were, at a rough count, three dozen Archbishops of Canterbury and probably more around the corner.

The Chaplain, who had been busy scribbling, glanced at the images, gave a wry smile and returned to his script. By now the crowds were pressing around the car. Many carried little flags which they waved furiously. The diligent Chaplain glanced up from his labours once again and squinted at a street trader carrying a tray of colourful objects. 'Good heavens,' he exclaimed, 'just look at that ... and THAT!'

He uttered the last word of his sentence with such ferocity that the driver jammed his foot on the brake and we were brought to an immediate halt in the midst of the teeming multitude.

The Chaplain gently lowered the window. His attention had been caught by two of the objects on sale. The first was clearly an item that had failed to sell out during the papal visit and was now on offer for the second time. It was a baseball cap carrying the inscription, *Welcome to the Holly Father*.

The Chaplain was a collector of hats, ecclesiastical and civil, and was reputed to be writing an authoritative work on the history of headgear. 'An intriguing inter-relationship between St Nicholas and the Bishop of Rome,' he muttered, as he pressed a coin into the hand of the vendor and took a cap for his collection.

He declined the second item, which was a balloon bearing the image of our employer. The intelligent vendor of this unusual novelty displayed a little card on which was written, 'Support the Anglican Communion and blow up the Archbishop of Canterbury.'

'Very droll,' murmured the Chaplain as he rewound the window. 'Very droll indeed.'

We resumed our journey through the crowd and along the dry, dusty street towards the church, where the cars stopped. I shall not dwell unduly on the ensuing service. Such events (and there were many) were the special responsibility of the Chaplain who, with the utmost devotion to duty, endured many hours of acute boredom with reverence and decorum. If my attendance was not required at such times, I would take myself away to a quiet corner for 40 winks or speed ahead to the next happening to check final details. On this occasion I made my way back to the main street to take a closer look at the cut-out Runcie. It was a work of art. A photograph of the prelate had been blown up to life size and then affixed to thick cardboard.

'These are quite splendid,' said I to a beaming Nigerian gentleman who was having his photograph taken by the side of the great man. 'I've never seen anything like this before. Most original.'

The gentleman admitted that it was his idea. He knew it would be a success. I revealed my identity and requested one of the images to take back to Lambeth Palace. There was no problem. I could have several. No, I didn't need several. Two, then? No, one would be ideal. I half expected him to ask me if I would like it gift-wrapped, but perhaps gift-wrapping had not yet arrived in Nigeria. Instead he promised to have it shipped to London. I thanked him warmly and returned to the sweltering heat of the church building.

Several months later, the cardboard Runcie arrived at Lambeth. Once it had been admired by the members of staff fortunate enough not to have visited Nigeria with us, a problem arose. What were we to do with it? It would have been a pity to consign it to the basement along with the woven baskets, spears and other trophies collected overseas. It was, however, not the sort of object that could grace the main Drawing Room. A solution was found, and the image was placed behind a secret door in what was once the Archbishop's study.

This room, now used as a staff meeting room, housed a substantial collection of books – records of proceedings in the House of Lords extending back several generations and sundry works of reference. These tomes were rarely consulted, but they were finely bound and one had to admit they looked well. The secret door was set in the midst of these precious volumes and, in order for it to remain secret, it was disguised by having books painted on it. Beyond the secret door there was a small space leading to another door, which opened into the Chaplain's study. Much innocent amusement was afforded some members of the Archbishop's staff when certain visitors to the Palace were given the grand tour and shown the secret door. When it was gently opened to reveal a full-sized Archbishop ready to pounce, their surprise was wondrous to behold.

I digress. Back in Nigeria Dr Runcie was in full cry from the pulpit. He was delivering a sermon that he (and his staff) knew by heart. It was an old standby which featured the Lord, the Link and the Local. Unkind staff members had dubbed the address 'The Lord, the Link and the Loony', but this was a joke in doubtful taste and perhaps I ought not to have included it here. The central theme was that the activities of the Christian community in the locality were all-important. It contained the memorable sentence, 'Nothing is real unless it is local.'

From time to time an inquisitive member of staff would ask what exactly Dr Runcie's definition of reality was. Quite properly, the Archbishop would point out that he did not enter the pulpit to baffle his listeners with obtuse philosophical speculation. People knew what he was getting at and that was all that was important. As far as I could make out, his judgement was perfectly accurate and the sermon was always extremely popular with everyone – except the staff, that is, who accepted it with the bored cynicism that is so typical of those who have become overfamiliar with greatness.

The Chaplain was sitting high in the sanctuary with a look of rapt attention on his perspiring face. He appeared to be the very model of Christian patience and humility. Dr Runcie brought his address to the conclusion we all anticipated and descended into the body of the church. A brass band especially convened for the service struck up and without more ado Dr Runcie, Archbishop Timothy and the Chaplain, together with a cast of hundreds, set off to process to the great West Door.

Processions are always welcome in church. They provide an amusing diversion for those who find sermons too exacting. They also provide the participants in the procession with an opportunity to exchange a few last-minute instructions. Archbishop Timothy, a very senior Archbishop, had processed for miles in his time and had mastered the art of singing a hymn, nodding to his friends (and enemies) in the congregation and issuing instructions to his Chaplain, all at the same time. Today he added to these impressive skills by maintaining a conversation with Dr Runcie. It was none too easy for His Grace of Canterbury to decipher the message, as Nigerian congregations, especially when boosted by a brass band, tend to neglect *piano* in favour of considerable volume, *fortissimo* for preference.

'*When you*—' began Timothy, 'Immortal, invisible, God only – *get to the* – hid from our eyes – *Great West* – thy great – *Door* – name we praise—' By now Archbishop Runcie was thoroughly confused. It was then that, once again, the value of a Chaplain was demonstrated.

22

'He says,' intervened the Chaplain in a stage whisper that would have disturbed John Peel, let alone the dead, 'he says, when you get to the West Door, will you go through it and bless the town?'

Archbishop Runcie nodded. He could not compete with Timothy in the processional conversation stakes and besides, he rather liked to sing this fine old hymn. There was plenty of time for His Grace to enjoy his vocal exercise, for as soon as the procession arrived at the West Door the band struck up yet again and off they went for another circuit of the building. After three complete turns, during which the faithful fell on their knees as the procession passed and the opportunists stretched out to touch the good Doctor, they arrived at that now familiar station, the Great West Door. The portals were thrown open and Dr Runcie, magnificent in his lightweight cope and mitre, lifted his hands towards the heavens.

At that very moment there was an almighty crash. The crowds both inside and outside the building let out a great shout. A large raindrop fell on Dr Runcie's outstretched hand, followed by another and another. The crowd began to cheer. Dr Runcie waved. They waved back. Infants who were witnessing rain for the first time in their lives were thrust towards the great rainmaker.

Archbishop Timothy was visibly moved. 'You will never be forgotten in these parts, Your Grace. Never.'

Dr Runcie remained silent as he contemplated the remarkable scene before him.

Well, I thought, as I stood in the shadows witnessing this contemporary miracle, perhaps the Anglican Communion in

Nigeria will grow at an even faster rate after today. As Dr Runcie so frequently and correctly reiterated, nothing is real unless it is local.

2

North of the Border

The Primus of Scotland is not, as some hikers might fondly imagine, a device for brewing a refreshing cup of tea during a walking tour of the Highlands. It is the designation enjoyed by the Bishop of the Episcopal Church in Scotland, who occupies the same position of supremacy as the Archbishop south of the border. There are important differences between the two, of course. Thanks to fiery characters such as John Knox, the Church established by law in Scotland is in fact the Presbyterian Church, and the supremo of that august body is known as the Moderator. The Church so established in England is, as we all know, the Church of England.

The Primus, elected by his brother bishops in Scotland, is the top dog within his own Church and occupies a position of equality alongside Archbishop Timothy and other archiepiscopal luminaries of the Anglican Communion. One further clarification before I proceed with my story: the main difference between His Grace of Canterbury and all the other Anglican Archbishops around the world is that Canterbury is recognized as *primus inter pares*. In short, this means that he is equal with the others but is always top of the class. That's it. No more definitions for the moment.

Our story concerning the Primus begins in Lambeth Palace. It was a summer afternoon and I had little desire to remain behind my desk in my office overlooking the front courtyard. I walked down the long corridor lined with oil paintings of former Archbishops. Records show that in the nineteenth century portraits by Holbein, Van Dyck, Kneller, Hogarth and Sir Joshua all hung in the Palace. There were evil rumours that since then many of the better paintings had been spirited away to grace other mansions. That may or may not be true, but there continue to be plenty of Archbishops at which the visitor may gaze.

Dr Runcie was fond of telling the story of how on one occasion he was conducting a distinguished group of Orthodox Bishops on a tour of the Palace. He took them along the corridor lined with pictures of his predecessors and into the Guard Room, full of yet more Primates. At the end of the excursion one of the bearded visitors thanked His Grace. 'Most interesting,' he intoned, 'but tell me, Archbishop, why are there no holy pictures?'

26

I turned right by an indifferent painting of Archbishop Ramsey and tapped on the Chaplain's door. His study, modest in its proportions, was adjacent to a larger room occupied by His Grace. At the entrance stood an old-fashioned hat stand festooned with headgear of every description. There was an ancient panama, which the Chaplain always took with him on his annual outing to Weymouth. (For reasons never divulged to me, he has a great affection for this English seaside town.) There was also a boater. The Chaplain was not an old Harrovian; in fact, he never wore the boater, but it looked well amongst the collection. A Canterbury cap, that shapeless symbol of Anglicanism, hung limply next to a stiff and starchy Roman biretta. My particular favourite was a broad-brimmed, black felt fedora of the type worn by Edward G. Robinson. I tried this particular hat on from time to time and thought that I looked rather good in it.

The Chaplain sat behind his desk, scribbling as usual. He gave me a cheery greeting as I entered. 'How are you?' I enquired in return.

'A walking miracle,' he responded. The Chaplain was given to making such endearing rejoinders. 'I imagine,' he continued, 'the weather being fine, you are anxious to quit your desk and take another jaunt to some remote part of the Communion. You know my views, don't you? Travel narrows the mind.'

He picked up his quill pen and began to address an envelope while I perched on the edge of his desk. 'You have friends over the water who appear to think as you do,' I said. 'The Archbishop is being attacked yet again for spending too much time abroad.'

27

I was referring to the inhabitants of the Mother of all Parliaments, namely the Palace of Westminster, which is directly opposite Lambeth Palace on the north bank of the Thames. The latest salvo to be fired into our garden from that building was in fact nothing more serious than a small squib. A junior MP, anxious to convince his constituents that he was a staunch defender of the faith, had complained that while His Grace was away, the nation was rapidly descending into moral anarchy, and only his constant presence could save the day. The staff at Lambeth were touched by the faith this particular MP showed in our employer.

The Chaplain returned his quill to its stand and sealed the envelope. 'It's happened before, my dear Terry. It will happen again. Archbishops have always provided would-be marksmen with target practice. It was often much rougher. You will recollect that Archbishop Alphege, some 1,000 years ago, was beaten to death with mutton bones?'

I had to confess that details of the unfortunate demise of Alphege were unknown to me. However, I remembered the story told about Michael Ramsey, a more recent holder of the office. On a visit to the United States, a cheeky reporter asked Archbishop Ramsey if he would be visiting any nightclubs during his stay. In a mild attempt at wit, the Archbishop retorted, 'Are there any nightclubs in New York?' – only to be dismayed the following morning when that very sentence was printed in the papers as the first question he had asked on arrival in the metropolis. Ramsey was not so accustomed to the sharpshooters of America. He was more at home with the double-barrelled shotguns deployed by the rustics of Westminster. He died, by the way, a peaceful death at a ripe old age, untroubled – as far as I know – by irate carnivores.

'As a matter of fact,' I said, 'we're due to make another trip very soon. The executive committee of the Anglican Consultative Council is planning to meet in Scotland.'

The Chaplain beamed. 'Splendid,' he said. 'I shan't be required for that particular junket and it's only next door. You might enjoy Scotland at this time of the year.'

I have already made mention of the organization known as the ACC. Although the Secretary General had his office in London, meetings of the group took place in great secrecy throughout the world. The secrecy was not by design. It simply happened. The lot, as they say, had now fallen on Scotland to host the Executive Council and the good Primus was going to try to introduce both the Archbishop and the foreign members of the Council to the Scottish Episcopalians.

The visit was not troublesome to organize. The appropriately named John Brown was going to drive us to a conference house in Scotland, where the Archbishop would meet with the Council members and also take one or two excursions into the territory occupied by the minority Episcopal Church.

The visit was duly announced and there were no rumbles from across the water, presumably because, strictly speaking, Scotland was not overseas and MPs doubtless considered that the Archbishop had every right to roam north of the border, improving the moral tone of the place in the process.

The Primus was on hand to greet the Archbishop on arrival. Unlike Nigeria, there was no bunting on display, nor were the streets lined with rapidly expanding Anglicans.

Instead, as befitted sparsely populated Scotland, there was the Primus, alone, suitably dressed for the occasion in grey trousers and a dapper tweed jacket. I was once informed that this good man never wore trousers until he was 12 years of age. As a youth he always sported the kilt, although once he assumed episcopal status he never wore it again.

The Primus of Scotland was a man of distinctive good humour and considerable dignity. Although he was always conscious of heading a Church that was numerically challenged, this did not deter him from playing a full and active international role. He had no worry about snipers. He could leave Scotland with impunity, and frequently did so to chair the ACC, or to stir up the World Council of Churches when they met in Bangkok or some other far-flung location.

'Welcome, Robert,' he said as he ushered us into the conference house. 'This is going to be a low-key visit. We want you to have a bit of a holiday and enjoy some rest up here.'

The Archbishop was gratified. It had been a demanding few weeks in London. The General Synod had required a week of his time in Church House, with clergy pensions being the main item on the agenda. He had then to deal personally with several major disputes in Canterbury – and had it not been for his timely intervention, fisticuffs might have resulted. Back at Lambeth, he had been faced with the acute problem of how to arrange the portraits of his predecessors for display in the Palace. The majority of the paintings were acceptable, but one or two of the more recent artists had clearly spent too long in the hot sun without a hat or had been overinfluenced by Picasso. Not that His Grace bore any grudge against that acknowledged artist; he simply felt that portraits in the classical tradition were more appropriate for hanging in the Long Gallery.

'I'm delighted to be here to enjoy some quiet,' said the Archbishop as he entered the main reception hall of the conference centre. Several secret members of the ACC, who had been lurking in the shadows pretending to be inconspicuous but secretly hoping to be the first to catch sight of the head of their Communion, leapt into sight and bore down on their visitor.

'G'day, Archbishop,' said a sober-looking Australian who sprang out of an armchair like a startled kangaroo. 'I was just this moment reading a report on the pensions debate. Pretty strong stuff.'

Before the Archbishop could reply, a matronly figure appeared from behind the long velvet curtains. 'Why, Dr Runcie, what a lovely surprise!' she exclaimed. Dr Runcie recognized her as one of the leading proponents of women's ordination in the USA. She was not to be trifled with, as she knew personally every Bishop in the States. Had she been allowed out to roam the Scottish countryside, her beguiling Southern accent would have charmed every Presbyterian minister from the severity of his own Communion into the comforting ranks of the Episcopal Church.

Just as the Archbishop was about to open his mouth, an Asian figure popped into sight, apparently from under the table. 'Good heavens!' said the startled Dr Runcie. 'I see everyone has assembled from across the globe.'

By now the room was swarming with the secret agents of the ACC who had appeared from every nook and cranny. Cups of tea were handed round and the American matron offered Dr Runcie a fairy cake, which he accepted, the food being perfectly safe in Scotland.

Before Dr Runcie could take a bite, however, he felt someone grasp his elbow and breathe American words of greeting in his good ear. Dr Runcie swivelled his head and recognized the Secretary General of the Secret Organization. 'Sam, how very good to see you,' he said, as strong tea slopped into his saucer. 'We haven't met since our discussion prior to my visit to Nigeria.'

The Secretary General was ideally suited to the position that he occupied. Diplomacy came as easily to him as slopping tea comes to the rest of us. 'I hear from Terry that you had a busy time in Africa,' Sam remarked, as he removed the Archbishop's cup and saucer and provided him with replacements.

'Busy time,' repeated Dr Runcie. 'You can say that again!'

'Yes,' said the Revd Sam, always ready to listen to and act on advice, 'I hear it was a very busy time.'

'I should tell you about our dinner with Governor Jim,' said the Archbishop, remembering a State Governor who had entertained us. 'He modelled himself on Kennedy, you know. When he came into dinner everyone stood and shouted, "Jeeeem! Jeeeem!" He was a powerful operator, I can tell you.'

By now Dr Runcie was laughing so much at these happy memories that he slopped his second cup of tea, leaving the Revd Sam to signal across the room for fresh supplies. A third cup of tea was produced and Sam offered it to His Grace. 'Do you have a full agenda this time?' queried the Archbishop, recollecting the past week with the Synod.

'We have to get quite a lot in,' said Sam. 'If we bring people from all over the world, we need to do as much as possible.'

The Archbishop held tightly onto his cup and nodded as a delegate clad in trainers and running shorts passed through the room *en route* to his daily evening run. I sidled up to Dr Runcie. 'It might not be a bad idea to get to your room and unpack,' I said. 'It appears there's going to be quite a deal of geniality during the next few days and we shall need all the strength we can muster.' He agreed with me and we started to move across the room, only to be stopped immediately by someone he had met in one of the remoter parts of New Zealand.

During my journeys I have observed the different techniques deployed by those with responsibility for seeing that the great and the good move, on time, from point A to point B. Some aides give the gentlest of touches to the elbow of their charge, hoping that he or she will respond like a small dinghy to a touch on the tiller. Some of the great – the royal great, for example – refuse to be touched and their aides have to resort to hand signals, eye contact or polite intervention when a natural break occurs in conversation.

Alas, like the economy, the great are frequently, if not always, a law unto themselves. Archbishop Runcie, as I have mentioned, was desirous of being charming to everyone he met. Even though he knew he had to be out of a room and into a car within three minutes, he could never resist stopping and having a personal discussion with every individual in his path. There were occasions when it took some three-quarters of an hour simply to cross a medium-sized reception room.

Reluctantly he would allow himself to be guided by the touch-on-the-elbow technique. There was only one occasion when the Chaplain and I went further than this, and not surprisingly it was in the fastest growing part of the Anglican Communion. At one point, the press of the Nigerian crowds being so great, there was a real concern that His Grace would be in actual danger of being torn limb from limb. As both the Chaplain and I stood well over six feet tall, we were able to use techniques generally considered inappropriate, and His Grace was saved to preach another day.

Such techniques were out of the question now, of course, even though it seemed advisable to leave the tea party without delay. The Archbishop was deep in conversation about that delicacy unique to New Zealand, the mutton bird (a smoked, bony titbit rather like an inferior kipper), when another delegate, this time from South America, sidled up and stood awaiting his opportunity to converse. There was nothing I could do. We left the room exactly 45 minutes later.

The Archbishop went to his modest room and I to mine. As neither of us had brought (or even possessed) running shoes, we agreed to take a short walk through the small town before dinner. We met as planned in the driveway. Inside the building delegates had gathered in small groups to thrash out some matter of vital importance to global Anglicanism. The Revd Sam required them to be very industrious during their clandestine meetings.

The Archbishop had changed from his dark clerical suit into his favourite, rust-coloured sweater. Although he claimed Scottish ancestry and had served with considerable distinction in the Scots Guards, no one would have taken him for a Scotsman. After all, he was born in Liverpool.

We set off at a gentle pace towards the town. On our right was the impressive pile of the cathedral, stripped of graven images many years previously and now controlled by the formidable Presbyterians. It was a mild evening and we were in good humour. At such times the Archbishop was an amiable and amusing companion. As we strolled on, he reminisced about his youth and told me how much he had enjoyed the *Beano* and the *Dandy* long before he became immersed in classical studies. Just as we were about to share recollections of *The Boy's Own Paper*, we espied a figure in the distance approaching us.

During our few hours in Scotland we had conversed and met with individuals from every part of the globe, but here was our first real Scotsman (the Primus excepted, of course). I made that assumption as we could clearly see that he was wearing the kilt.

As he drew closer, we noted that the man was observing us with some interest. When he was but a few yards away, he stopped and stared at me. We stopped too. The Primate of All England (in disguise) bade him a good evening. The Scotsman did not reply. He remained staring at me.

After several more moments of silence, he opened his mouth. 'Mr Waite,' he said in a broad Scottish accent.

'That's right,' I replied.

'I didna expect to see ye in Scotland. Come and have a wee dram and bring yer friend along too.'

Dr Runcie gave a wee smile. I waited a moment before replying. I remembered that we were in Scotland, a proud

Presbyterian nation where Bishops and their kin were hardly treated with the respect that one might expect to be accorded to those who followed so closely in the footsteps of the apostles. Was the kilted fellow deliberately ignoring an Episcopalian?

'May I introduce my friend?' I said genially.

'Ay,' replied the Scotsman.

'This,' I said, 'is Dr Robert Runcie, Archbishop of Canterbury and Primate of All England.' (I must confess that I added the latter part of the sentence out of pure mischief.)

The Scotsman pondered this statement. 'All England, ye say? Runcie, is it? A Scots name. Did ye know that that fellow up there—' he pointed towards the roof of the cathedral, '—that fellow who cleans the moss off the tiles and keeps the gutters clear is named Runcie?'

He cupped his hands around his mouth and bellowed in the general direction of the roof. 'Runcie! Come on down and meet your own kith and kin!'

Runcie on the roof appeared from behind a pillar and gave a cheery wave. We waved back. 'He'll no come doon,' said the Scotsman. 'It's a long way, even if it is a relative who wants to see him.'

We thanked the Scotsman for his kind offer of a drink, which we declined due to shortage of time, and bade him a friendly farewell. As we retraced our steps, the Archbishop fell into reflective mood. 'You remember what Henry James said of Scotland?' he asked, revealing that his knowledge of literature extended way beyond the *Beano*.

I confessed that I did not.

'He said that once you get the hang of it, it's a most beautiful and admirable little country. One might say the same about the people.'

'Ay,' I said. 'It's also been called the knuckle-end of England. We'd better get back for supper before we meet the men with mutton bones.'

* * * * *

The days spent with the Anglican Consultative Council in Scotland passed slowly. The Revd Sam, with his usual devotion to duty, made sure that every waking moment was fully occupied and it was with some considerable relief that on the final evening before our departure the Primus introduced a diversion. He decided that he ought to summon a group of notable Scottish Episcopalians to meet with his brother Archbishop and members of the ACC. The location for this jolly gathering was the local Hydro, the Hydro being a hotel of sizeable proportions perched on a hill above the town. After an exhausting week, members of the conference were looking forward to spending a night on the town at the expense of their host.

As is often the case in Scotland, on the evening of the outing it was raining heavily. Heavy rain there means the sort of downpour that caused Noah to look for his carpenter's kit and send his wife to round up the animals. A car was provided for Dr Runcie and he and I, together with the good Primus, set off up the hill. The driver pulled up outside the front entrance of the hotel. It was pitch black. As we wiped the mist off the car windows and peered through the gloom, the lobby appeared like a Presbyterian church on a weekday – firmly secured. There was not a soul in sight.

'I don't understand,' said the Primus. 'The whole building is in darkness.' The Primus was a truthful man and, as two Archbishops do not constitute a Lambeth Conference, there was no dispute.

'Drive to the side door,' instructed our host.

The driver put the car into gear and proceeded around the side of the building, narrowly missing a concrete mixer and several piles of what appeared to be old carpeting and redundant kitchen equipment.

'Oh dear, oh dear,' muttered the Primus. 'I don't very much like the look of this.'

After driving between two or three heaps of sand and a small crane, we arrived at the side door. By the lights of the car we could make out a lone figure wrestling with an umbrella as the wind attempted to tear it from his grasp. The Primus lowered the window.

'Is there a problem?' he enquired.

The wretched figure approached the vehicle. 'Problem?' he said, quite forgetting to bid the head of the Episcopal Church in Scotland a good evening. 'Problem? You can say that again.'

The Primus, not being one to waste words, did not take up the invitation.

'We're in the middle of major renovations,' the dripping doorman went on. 'There's flooding in the building. Now the power has failed. Your party is in one of the upper rooms.'

The Primus, no doubt considering that an upper room was a most suitable location for his group, indicated that we would join them. Still wrestling with his umbrella, the door-man grasped the handle of the car door and pulled it open. A minor tidal wave swept across the back seat.

Like drowning seamen heading for a lifeboat, the clerical party leapt into the night and stumbled towards the hotel door. 'Damn this lock,' muttered the doorman, as he attempted to shelter his charges under his tattered umbrella and open the door at the same time. A sudden gust of wind swept the umbrella from his grip, exposing everyone to the deluge.

'I'll open this if it's the last thing I do,' promised our increasingly desperate guide. He gave a huge pull on the han-dle and mercifully the door flew open, revealing what appeared to be the entrance to an underground cavern.

'Go carefully,' he instructed. 'There's some water about and a bit of building work. Continue until you come to the lift.'

There was a great deal of water sloshing around on the floor of the cavern. We paddled in the general direction of a dim emer-gency light and as we proceeded through the gloom, we heard what appeared to be the sound of a mighty waterfall. We arrived at the lift entrance, the lights flickered and suddenly all was illu-minated as the power returned, to reveal two dripping Primates in the midst of what appeared to be an underground lake.

'The water's running down the lift shaft, Robert,' observed the Primus. He was correct again. A considerable volume of water was running down the shaft. It was rather like being trapped in a flooded coal mine.

'It is indeed,' replied Dr Runcie. In an attempt to intro-duce some humour into the situation he added, 'But after all, this is a Hydro.'

I leaned forward and pressed the button to call the elevator, only to leap back immediately as I received a sharp electric shock for my troubles. Dr Runcie, a veteran of World War II and a survivor of Archbishop Timothy's Nigeria, remained calm. The elevator door opened, we entered and I gingerly pressed the button. We ascended to the next floor without incident.

A small party of Episcopalians were sipping a rather insipid-looking white wine in the upper room and drying out in the process. I recognized some members of the ACC lurking in the dark corners. The Revd Sam was busy attempting to inject some jollity into the occasion. 'Why, hello Your Grace! Hello, Primus! A little wet tonight, but never mind.' The Revd Sam was unfailingly cheerful, which is probably why he was given one of the most difficult jobs in the Communion.

I cast my eyes around the room, looking for signs of further trouble. My heart sank when at the back of the room I glimpsed a slide projector. 'What's that for, Sam?' I asked, as he finished pouring an orange juice for a stout lady in a tweed hat.

'The Scottish Church Communication Department is going to show us what church life in Scotland is like,' said Sam, jovial as ever. 'We shall all need to be seated in a moment. You're next to the Archbishop in the front row.'

I made my dismal way towards a hard chair. All around there was the steady hum of electric fan heaters as a vain attempt was made to dry the room and its occupants. It was clearly an impossible task. The air was thick with the smell of drying tweed.

We sat facing the screen. The Primus stood before us, welcomed everyone and congratulated members of his flock, many of whom had travelled considerable distances in order to meet Archbishop Runcie and members of the ACC Special Boat Squad. He then took his seat and the lights dimmed, this time following instructions from the communication expert rather than by an act of God. There was a loud click and Scottish Episcopal music boomed from a tape recorder.

I feel that it would be kinder to our hosts of that memorable evening to pass over the next half-hour. We would do better to reflect on sentiments expressed by Rudyard Kipling, who recommended that triumph and disaster be treated as similar impostors. There is no reason to go calling the evening a failure simply because the communication expert inserted every other slide into the projector upside down and there were several further power cuts, which plunged the room into both silence and darkness. The fact that dampness had so affected the slides that the skilful operator of the magic lantern found it totally impossible to focus a single one correctly is certainly no reflection whatsoever on the state of modern technology in Episcopal Scotland. Not at all.

The evening drew to its soggy end. The Special Boat Squad left early. The hardy Scots pulled on their wellington boots and prepared for the long journey home. The Revd Sam congratulated the lantern operator. Dr Runcie braced himself for the morrow. It had been a Scottish night to remember.

* * * * *

As is so often the case after a stormy night, the following morning was bright and cheerful. John Brown appeared at the appointed time and I tapped on the door of Dr Runcie's bedroom. He was engaged in a rather fearsome tussle with a pair of socks and a dressing gown, which refused to confine themselves to his suitcase. A few smart blows on the lid of the case, followed by a manoeuvre that I had learned from watching all-in wrestling on television, quickly brought them to submission and John carted the case off to the boot of the car.

We had said farewell to the Revd Sam and his squad at breakfast and told them all how much we looked forward to meeting them again in Nigeria. For diplomatic reasons, yet to be disclosed, the Revd Sam had selected Nigeria as the location of the next full meeting of the ACC. Even though the gathering was a year or so in the future, I experienced a chill of apprehension, despite the fact that the Scottish sun was as warm as could be expected for the time of year.

The American matron was the last to bid us farewell. As she clasped the hand of Dr Runcie, there were tears of emotion in her Southern eyes. Dr Runcie urged her not to be distressed. We would all certainly meet again when he visited the United States and, if not then, we could still look forward to the day when the last trump would sound and there would be great rejoicing as we met old friends and forgave old enemies.

Alas, I must confess that Dr Runcie did not in fact utter the latter part of this statement. I have made it up simply because one might imagine it to be the sort of thing an Archbishop ought to say – but then, Dr Runcie did not always conform to type.

John Brown put the stretched Ford into gear and we moved away. The Archbishop turned to me. 'Where next?' he asked.

His Grace knew very well where we were going, but from time to time he liked to test his staff to see that they were on top of events. I told him that we were on our way to a Scottish university where he was to deliver an address, after which we were going to lunch with the newly appointed Moderator of the Church of Scotland. Dr Runcie nodded. Once he had delivered his oration, the day would be reasonably relaxed. All very satisfactory. He lay back and closed his eyes.

We duly arrived at the university. Dr Runcie was greeted warmly and lectured with competence and style for an hour or so. There was no time for a reception following the lecture, as John Brown was obliged to drive to the official house of the Moderator so that bread might be broken between the two Churchmen. We left the lecture theatre to walk the short distance to the car. As we approached the vehicle I noticed a group of a dozen or so individuals standing alongside. Several of the group carried placards, on which were written various diverse and pointed slogans. One surly little fellow brandished a board proclaiming, 'Runcie is a Papist'. Another urged Bishops to keep well away from the Highlands and Lowlands of Scotland.

'A small farewell party, I see,' said the Archbishop to the Vice Chancellor.

'I'm afraid it's the Revd Jack Glass, Sir,' retorted our host. 'We were half expecting him to burst into the lecture theatre. He spared us that and I don't expect he will be too troublesome now.'

As observant readers will have gathered from the slogans, the Revd Glass and his supporters inclined towards the Protestant side of religion. As Ian Paisley was to Ireland, so the

Revd Jack was to Scotland. He perceived Dr Runcie as having leanings towards Rome. This did not win the Archbishop many marks with Jack and his lads, who were determined to let it be known that the great beast of Rome and his friends would be hunted down at every available opportunity. Apart from that, as I have mentioned, Bishops could be given a bit of a roasting in Scotland from time to time anyway, and Jack was a dab hand with the barbecue.

Dr Runcie proceeded fearlessly towards the car. Jack moved to intercept him. 'Good morning, Jack,' said the Archbishop politely. The two had met on several previous occasions and, in fairness to the Revd Glass, it must be said that in private conversation, though vigorous in argument, he was courteous in behaviour. In public he often adopted a more belligerent style.

'You're an appeaser, Runcie!' shouted Glass now. 'A traitor to your heritage. Protestants died for their faith. What right have you to sell that down the river? You're no better than a Judas. You're a friend of the beast!'

As he uttered the final words of his dramatic denunciation, he rummaged in his pocket and produced a packet of silver 20-pence pieces, which he held out for Dr Runcie to accept. 'Take these, you Judas!' he spluttered.

The Archbishop did not stretch out his hands to receive the silver and in a gesture of disgust the fiery Jack cast the money at the feet of the lesser beast of Canterbury. 'There,' he said triumphantly. 'There's your thirty pieces of silver.'

Dr Runcie climbed into the car and I stooped down to retrieve the money. 'Thanks, Jack,' I said. 'Most considerate. It will come in very useful for the telephone.'

The Revd Jack looked stunned. 'You're not *taking* it, are ye?' he asked incredulously.

'Of course,' I replied. 'Drive on, John. We have an appointment in Edinburgh.'

Dr Runcie and I sat together in the back of the stretched Ford as we pulled away from the university. 'He's not a bad fellow, really,' said the Archbishop as he chuckled to himself. 'We've often spoken together, you know, but he tends to get a bit excited when he's on parade. Are we going to be on time, John?'

The competent John Brown assured us that we would be precisely on time unless something unforeseen happened. Precisely on time, therefore, we pulled up before the elegant official house of the newly elected Moderator of the Church of Scotland. The Moderator welcomed the great and the good of Edinburgh to his luncheon party that day, and this was when I realized that the Presbyterian Church is not quite as puritanical as I had imagined.

For a start, the Moderator was dressed in his official kit, which was quite splendid: frock coat, knee britches, silk stockings and buckled shoes. 'How's that for a show to rival the Anglicans?' I thought. We climbed the stairs to an upper reception room where drinks were served. None of your orange juice and insipid white wine here. We were presented with a glass of the finest malt whisky. To this day I can still remember its aroma and deliciously smooth flavour. It was a gentle and fitting conclusion to a visit that had not been without its moments of stress.

Eventually we said our farewells and made our way downstairs to the car. Was it Milton who said that the New

Presbyter is but old Priest writ large? Perhaps I have taken him out of context, but Piskie, Presby or what have you, we all have our own distinctive plumage. When it comes to the aroma of sanctity, however, our established brothers and sisters north of the border certainly have the edge on us.

3

VIP Treatment

When travelling alone I have found it instructive, and frequently salutary, to reflect on the sayings of great men and women. One harbours the vain thought that in years to come, travellers in outer space might peruse this very volume in order to find inspiration during their long voyage to the edge of the universe (assuming, of course, that the universe has an 'edge').

The recorded utterances of the great and the good vary considerably. Some have the immediate clarity of pure spring water. Others may be equally refreshing once they have been distilled and allowed to mature for a while. Take the following, for example: 'Never take a cold bath in Africa, unless ordered to do so by a doctor.' Such was the suggestion in *Hints to*

Travellers, offered by Dr William Henry Cross in 1906.

If the innocent traveller were to accept this hint without question, he could easily find himself going without a bath of any kind for a considerable period of time, hot water being a rare commodity in

> *that mysterious land!*
> *Surrounded by a lot of sand*
> *and full of grass and trees.*

Hilaire Belloc described it thus in 1898. I admit, things may have changed since then, but Belloc, in poetic mood, captures something of the Africa travellers know and love, the land where a bath of any description is welcome. As you may have gathered, I am still distilling the remarks of Dr Cross.

It is up to the truly great names to speak with clarity and purity: 'In Africa think big.' Now that is water from the spring – clear, sparkling, refreshing and spoken by none other than the renowned Cecil Rhodes.

I had occasion to reflect on this profound statement when attempting to travel from Lagos in the west of the continent to Cape Town in the south. The Archbishop and his trusty Chaplain were safely ensconced in Lambeth Palace, attending to urgent domestic matters and keeping an eye on Westminster across the water. I was out and about in the world, preparing for future visits throughout the Anglican Communion. After exertions that would reduce the labours of Hercules to a mere picnic, I managed to travel from the centre of Lagos to the airport.

Once there, I concluded at first that I had somehow chosen to travel on a day when the entire Islamic population was bound for Mecca, Christians for the Holy Land and the remainder for any part of the world that would accept them. I was wrong. It was a normal day in Nigeria. Everyone wanted out, as the saying goes. Given the fact that the International Terminal was teeming with life and hand-to-hand fighting was breaking out in front of most of the ticket counters, the airline officials appeared remarkably serene.

Obtaining my ticket was a tedious business that involved mediating sundry potentially serious disputes, plotting my path through several tons of hand luggage and encountering airline staff who were so relaxed that they claimed they had no record whatsoever of my ever having booked a ticket. This latter fact was hardly surprising as all computers in the building had been out of action throughout the afternoon, enabling the staff to enjoy their serenity in the midst of what was not much short of a minor civil war.

As evening fell, the busy world was far from hushed and agitated travellers continued to be plagued by the fever of life, which was rapidly developing into a battle for survival. In short, no work had been done and I remained stranded. Then, in the twinkling of an eye, all – well, almost all – was resolved. The computers flickered into action, the staff yawned into sluggish activity and renewed fighting broke out throughout the concourse. My ticket was duly delivered and I prepared for the hazardous journey through customs and immigration. I shall pass over that prolonged and frustrating experience. The memory of it still distresses me and I have no desire to pass on that grief to the reader, especially if he or she be on their lonely way to the edge of space.

I felt a small twinge of anxiety when, in the relative peace of the departure lounge, I examined my ticket. I was booked to travel from Nigeria to Zaire and then onwards to South Africa. In Zaire there were just two hours to wait for my onward connection. Travellers will know too well that Western and African concepts of time do not always harmonize. When Lord Hemingford remarked that in Africa it is always five minutes to 12, he may have been expressing what I am trying to convey. Suffice to say, time and timetables can be a problem for the Western traveller in the continent of Africa. Unlike the noble Lord's clock, I was alarmed.

The journey to Zaire passed pleasantly enough. At one point there was a minor commotion at the back of the plane when a thirsty traveller produced a spirit stove and prepared to brew a pot of tea. Fortunately he was restrained by members of the same group who had fought with such determination in the terminal concourse, and we landed safely.

'Fatal Africa,' observed the great Henry Morton Stanley. 'One after another travellers drop away.' How right he was, I thought, when only two passengers disembarked in Zaire – a youngish man dressed in blue jeans and a check shirt, and myself. We crossed the tarmac together and were mercifully reunited with our luggage. Compared to Lagos, the terminal in Zaire was a haven of tranquillity. It was so peaceful, in fact, that we began to feel somewhat nervous. We stumbled across the dimly lit departure lounge, looking for a place to book in for our next flight. Not one booth was illuminated. Our feelings of apprehension increased, as not only had all the travellers disappeared, but seemingly everyone else had too.

The man in the colourful shirt (a seasoned traveller and, I was later to discover, a very important man in the business world) suggested that I guard the luggage while he went off to try to find some sign of life. I glanced at my watch. Our plane was due to leave in half an hour.

After five minutes or so, my companion returned. 'Bad news,' he said.

I confessed that I was hardly surprised.

'There's a war on,' he explained. 'Our connecting flight arrived early and, because of possible trouble, departed immediately.'

I could see our speed downhill was increasing rapidly.

'The next flight is in three days. It's useless to try to get into town. Apart from being too dangerous, every hotel is occupied by journalists.'

In times of crisis, when one feels the need to gain inspiration from the sayings of the great, it is important to be selective. Stanley, after noting how his companions in Africa disappeared, went on to speak about 'the rabid fury of the native guarding every entry and exit, the unspeakable misery of life within the wild continent, the utter absence of every comfort, the bitterness which each day heaps upon the poor white man's head...' Clearly, at this juncture, Stanley was not our man, but good old Rhodes was: 'In Africa think big.'

While my new-found companion was what might be called casually dressed, I – although only occupying a lowly position as a junior layman in the Church of England – was quite the opposite, as I was due to be met in South Africa by an Archdeacon, and Archdeacons, as guardians of Church fabric, know a thing or two about sartorial elegance.

'Come,' I commanded confidently. 'I shall be a most important traveller; a VIP, in fact. You, dressed as you are, must take on the role of my bodyguard.'

We picked up our cases and set off to explore the dark hinterland of the terminal. Those who frequent airports will have noted that, whenever a new building is designed, the architect is given one instruction that must be followed come what may. This is that every arriving and departing passenger must be made to walk as far as possible. We walked along deserted corridors, across empty departure halls and through vacant offices. The campaign that day had been hard fought and after half an hour or so we were feeling somewhat tired and dispirited when, to our delight, we met another human being.

Unlike the great Livingstone and Stanley in the most famous encounter in African history, the man we met was certainly not looking for us, nor did he seem especially pleased to see us. In order to gain an immediate advantage, and in keeping with the military spirit of the day, I quickly threw him a command. 'Please take us immediately to the VIP lounge.'

He looked at me and then took a longer look at my casual companion. 'That's my bodyguard. He must stay by my side at all times.'

The lone figure turned and we followed. Even VIPs are not exempt from the architect's rule, and after a hike of 15 minutes or so we arrived outside a splendid private lounge.

'Where is the book?' I demanded in a polite but firm tone. The lonely man, who seemed to know everything, produced a leather-bound volume and we inscribed our names therein. 'If we do that now,' I said *sotto voce* to my bodyguard, 'they won't throw us out in the morning. Once you're in the book, you're in.'

By now my newly appointed bodyguard was thinking along the same lines as Cecil Rhodes. 'Mr Waite will need some food,' he said. 'We shall also need something to drink.'

The lonely man looked abashed. 'I shall need money,' he muttered.

'No problem,' said the bodyguard. He rummaged in his briefcase and produced a little box. He opened it, revealing at least two dozen miniature Swiss Army penknives. 'Take these,' he said. 'We have no money, but plenty of these.'

For the first time that evening the lonely man smiled. He accepted one of the penknives, disappeared and returned within 30 minutes with an old-fashioned 10 Downing Street lunch – namely beer and sandwiches.

We spent the next three days in the VIP lounge, eating and drinking like real VIPs thanks to our little stock of knives. At 4 o'clock on the third and final morning, our slumbers were disturbed by a posse of military men with instructions to search the room. As our names were 'in the book', we were safe. We returned to sleep, only to be awakened some two hours later by a visit from none other than the President of the Republic, who was on his way to the battle zone. I chatted pleasantly enough with him, as VIPs do, while my bodyguard lurked in the corner of the room with half a dozen gun-toting bruisers. Finally, after a refreshing early-morning beer or two, the President departed, and later that morning we also left.

As I flew across that great continent *en route* to Cape Town, there was time to ponder further on the wisdom of Rhodes, in particular his expansive thinking. At least, I thought, think as big as you can, given the limitations of the situation, and if you can't think big enough, perhaps a miniature Swiss Army knife might help you survive for a day or so, even if you don't win every round of the battle – and you never will, in Africa.

4

The Hog Farm

'The Bronx. No thonx.' So said Ogden Nash. 'USA. No way,' was my own less than worthy feeling when it was suggested that a visit to the Episcopal Church in the United States ought to be arranged.

It was not that I disliked the United States. Far from it. I first visited that vast country as a young man and was greatly appreciative of the generosity I experienced there. In fact, I first met the Revd Sam in New York. He was labouring away in the Head Office of the Episcopal Church on Second Avenue. His task in those days was to see that American Churchmen around the world were properly cared for. This particular work demanded not only diplomatic skill but also considerable

stamina, as he frequently had to visit lone American missionaries toiling in some remote corner of the global vineyard.
Eventually he came to visit us in Uganda and brought us
news of others working in Japan, Southern Africa and South
America. He was a frequent visitor to these far-flung regions,
wherever the American Episcopal Church had interests.

My reservations about the USA were to do with the very size
of the country. Given the fact that so many MPs were anxious to
listen to Dr Runcie proclaim the Christian message throughout
the British Isles, clearly he could not be away for too long without doing damage to their immortal souls. America, being a
large country, would take a great deal of time to visit properly.

Before undertaking the journey to the New World, therefore, I consulted with our resident American in London, the
aforementioned Revd Sam. This was in the days before the
great silver auction and his office was still in desirable
Westminster. It was not too easy to find, because, you will recollect, there was a certain amount of secrecy surrounding the
Anglican Consultative Council. Those in the know, however,
could locate it easily enough.

I have frequently marvelled at the ability of certain individuals to convey the impression that you are the *only* person
they want to see that day. The Revd Sam was such a character.
He swept me into his cheerful office, radiating enthusiasm. The
walls were decorated with a few trophies marking his visits
to the Orient, where the American Church had considerable
interests. There were also several happy family photographs:
Sam with 400 bishops, Sam with His Grace of Canterbury, Sam
stepping into a taxi to meet with the Primus of Scotland and

his bishops (that is, I do not mean to suggest that the good Primus and his Episcopal merry men were all *in* the taxi – although, come to think of it, they might well have been, as there are not too many Anglican Bishops in Scotland).

Although an American through and through, Sam invariably adjusted to his immediate surroundings with ease. I have watched him eat mashed boiled banana in Kenya as though it were the staple food of New Yorkers. Therein, I would suggest, lies the secret of his great diplomatic ability – namely empathy.

'Have a cup of tea?' he said. Tea and digestive biscuits arrived immediately.

'How was the Scottish meeting?' I enquired. (Dr Runcie and I, of course, had left Sam's meeting early in order to dine with the Moderator.)

'Very good,' said Sam with redoubled enthusiasm. 'Wonderful spirit.'

I marvelled then as I marvel now. There are certain exceptional individuals in this troubled world who have an unusual ability to enjoy conferences. Sam was such a man. His enjoyment so conveyed itself to others that they too came away from discussing the New Zealand Prayer Book, or a fresh administrative region for the Church in Borneo, and (as it were) danced through the streets of Dundee.

'The next full meeting of the ACC will be in Nigeria as you know,' he said. 'They have a splendid new government conference centre, but more about that later. You're off to America soon, aren't you?'

I had seen many such government centres in Africa and needed some convincing of their attractiveness. Leaving such quibbles aside for the time being, however, I agreed that the United States was my concern at this particular moment.

'You can't go everywhere, obviously,' he said, 'but you must cover as much ground as possible – 815 will want a visit; you must go to rural America and, of course, to California. The White House should be on the programme also.'

The '815' to which the Revd Sam referred was not, as one might imagine, another secret HQ. It was the address on Second Avenue where the Episcopal Church in the United States had its main administrative office and above which the Presiding Bishop resided in a penthouse. (I should explain that the Presiding Bishop was the top man in the Episcopal Church, equal with such individuals as the Primus, Archbishop Timothy, and a host of other characters whom we have yet to encounter.)

We often hear that what America does today, the remainder of the world does tomorrow. There is a certain amount of truth in this statement. The Episcopal Church was first into the great auction business, and began to sell off the family heirlooms when ordinary folk still thought that a bailiff was but a rural farmworker in the old country. The magnificent residence and offices of the Presiding Bishop in Greenwich, Connecticut were rapidly disposed of in favour of 815. The poor old PB, as he was affectionately called, was forced to move to Second Avenue and live above the shop. Being a holy man, he accepted this change without complaint. 'Penthouse' may sound very grand, but in reality it was just a top-floor flat with a couple of guest rooms tacked on.

Fuelled by our tea and digestive biscuits, the Revd Sam and I roughed out a draft programme for the proposed archiepiscopal visit to the States. One year later, I sat with Dr

Runcie and his Chaplain in the much-maligned penthouse high above Second Avenue.

Generally speaking, in the days when it was my good fortune to travel with Dr Runcie, his fellow Archbishops throughout the world were a good-natured bunch. The PB in America was certainly one of the most amiable. I imagine that a certain theatrical ability is required in order to appear in church Sunday by Sunday and entertain the faithful, but the PB's real talent was displayed when, accompanied by none other than the Revd Sam on the piano, he performed a most acceptable rendering of the old song, 'In the five and ten cent store'. I hasten to add that he did not, of course, sing this ditty in church, but at private social gatherings. As he was certainly no show-off, he took not a little persuading to display his vocal talents, but when he did so it was always appreciated.

The PB was briefing us on the details of the programme that had been roughed out so long ago. 'We've included a visit I know you'll enjoy,' he said, as Dr Runcie stood on the balcony of the penthouse mopping his brow. It was very hot and humid. A fire engine ploughed its way through the evening rush-hour traffic making a noise like a wounded rhinoceros.

'It's a bit noisy out here,' observed the Archbishop, as the air-conditioning outlet blasted into action. We moved indoors and silence fell as the PB closed the triple-glazed doors. A noticeable chill descended on the room, as though by some miracle we had been transported to the territory covered by the Bishop of the Arctic.

'It's not easy to get the balance right,' said the PB as he fiddled with the air-conditioner. He gave up, settled into a comfortable sofa and returned to the matter in hand. 'The visit you'll enjoy is to a hog farm.'

Those who have stumbled across this book and are reading about the everyday life of Archbishops for the first time may be a little surprised that such a location would figure on a visit by His Grace to our American cousins. In fact, there should be no surprise. The Archbishop of Canterbury had a well-known fondness for pigs, Berkshires in particular. He claimed to have owned several of the species, and it was with a heavy heart that he gave them to a charity when the demands of office became too great.

My knowledge of hogs was certainly not as extensive as that of the Archbishop. It was limited to the days when, as a boy, I watched them being fed in my home village on a repulsive mixture known as Manchester Pudding. The mixture was composed of scraps collected from various hotels in the Manchester area. The scraps were boiled and then fed to the grateful swine in huge, evil-smelling chunks. From time to time, an item of cutlery from the Midland Hotel or another such grand establishment was discovered in the mix, and we would know who to blame for that week's appalling aroma.

The Archbishop duly expressed pleasure at the thoughtful inclusion of pigs in his itinerary, and the PB was gratified. The following morning we departed for rural America.

The hog farm we visited was on a somewhat grander scale that the humble establishment I had known in my youth. I remember from those days a makeshift little pen with a couple of porkers anxiously awaiting whatever fare the finest Manchester eating houses could provide. America, as ever, was bigger and better – a thousand times so.

When we landed at the airport, the hog farmer met us with his private helicopter. 'Hi!' he said cheerfully. To my untrained eye, he looked like a mid-western banker – and that, I discovered, was exactly what he was. He owned the largest hog farm in the country and the most prestigious bank in the state.

As we flew across the flatlands, he shouted information at us. The noise of the helicopter was such that it was only possible to catch occasional words. 'Automatic feed ... 20,000 every day ... world hunger ... hygiene...'

We nodded dutifully while the Chaplain scribbled away in a notebook. The hog farmer, imagining that he was taking notes, kept the information flowing. In fact, the Chaplain was conscious that on the morrow Dr Runcie had to deliver at least five major speeches, of which only three had so far been drafted. It was necessary for him to redeem the time, as they say.

The pilot of the helicopter circled. Below us we could see a complex that resembled one of the larger British holiday camps. We put down in the midst of the compound and were greeted by a whole group of porcine bankers. A hay cart had been decked out with some bunting and a microphone, and Dr Runcie was encouraged to clamber aboard and deliver some well-chosen words, which he did with his usual eloquence. There was a little polite applause and then a man approached us dressed as though he was about to perform major surgery. He was clad from head to toe in white; he wore a white cap and his features were cloaked in a white protective mask. I imagined that the hogs felt quite safe in his presence.

'You need to put these on,' he muttered through the gauze, while he handed us three pairs of white overalls. We obediently changed and were ushered towards a couple of electric golf carts for a tour of the establishment. We saw a lot of hogs, that I can guarantee. Clearly they were superior hogs, who had never heard of Manchester Pudding, let alone tasted it.

At the conclusion of the tour, the hog banker took us to one side for some refreshment. 'I have a scheme,' he said, 'that will change the world.' Dr Runcie looked interested, as changing the world was something dear to his heart. 'I want you, Archbishop,' the banker went on with a flourish, 'to take one of my best hogs to England. I want you, Archbishop, to breed that hog. I want you, Archbishop, to send lots of little hogs to Africa. If you do that, we will solve the problem of world hunger.'

The Archbishop needed no convincing. It was a good scheme. Feed a hog, breed a hog, and send the little ones to a warmer climate. There and then we went to see our hog, Martha.

Alas, it was several months before the plan could come to fruition. Bureaucrats can put the damper on the most promising of schemes. Who would need convincing that American hogs were in robust health? The Ministry. Who was reluctant to allow the finest hog in the world into England? The Ministry. Who insisted that the most wonderful hog in America had to spend months in quarantine? The Ministry. Finally, however, the great day dawned and Martha emerged from months of isolation into the welcoming company of His Grace of Canterbury. By now all the other archiepiscopal hogs had gone to be cared for elsewhere and Martha joined them. Never one to forget old friends, the Archbishop visited them frequently.

Sad to say, world hunger is still with us and no little archiepiscopal piglets ever saw the sunny shores of Africa. Why not? Well, Martha proved to be infertile. I do not know if this disastrous news was ever communicated to the hog banker in America. I suspect it may not have been. He meant well. Everyone meant well.

The Chaplain, always one to subject any scheme to the most cynical scrutiny, was not impressed. 'What,' he said, quoting an old proverb, 'what can you expect from a pig but a grunt?'

'Animals can be soothing,' I replied. 'Remember the limerick?'

> 'An Archbishop, to keep himself calm,
> Kept pigs on a Hertfordshire farm.
> The grunts and the snores
> Of the prize-winning boars
> To episcopal ears were as balm.'

The Chaplain did not grunt. He was too much of a gentleman for that. He simply returned to his scribbling without a further word.

* * * * *

Those who have followed these stories so far will have developed some familiarity with the Anglican Consultative Council. They will know that the ACC was composed of Bishops, clergy and laymen and -women from across the globe. They will further know that the one who ensured that the Council met on time and dutifully worked through its agenda was none other than the Revd Sam. I have hinted, too, that there was a slight air of secrecy about the Council. Any reader can test this simply by buttonholing an ordinary member of any Anglican church throughout the world and questioning them about the ACC. I guarantee you a blank look and shuffling of the feet.

There is, however, an even more clandestine body that congregates from time to time, and this is known as the Primates' Meeting. In Anglican circles the Primus of Scotland, Archbishop Timothy, the PB of America, His Grace of Canterbury and several others are all known as Primates. Every few years or so they meet together, with Canterbury in the chair and the Revd Sam in attendance, shuffling not his feet but a sheaf of papers.

During the travels of Dr Runcie through the New World, Primates from across the Communion had made their way to America and were planning to deliberate at the College of Preachers in Washington. Dr Runcie was due to join them for a day or so (provided he could tear himself away from the hogs).

The College of Preachers nestles in the shadow of what is called The National Cathedral in Washington. This impressive looking Anglican edifice is built along classical lines and attempts to play a significant role in American life similar to that played by Westminster Abbey or St Paul's Cathedral in the United Kingdom. The College of Preachers is not, as some cynics might fondly imagine, a contemporary manifestation of the Tower of Babel. It is a conference centre where, from time to time, clerics and others are instructed in the art of sermonizing. It is normally a place that I would avoid at all costs. Duty called, however.

By the time we arrived, the other Primates were well established and very much at home. They had flown in from across the globe and were being greeted by our genial and hospitable preaching hosts. I shall not dwell on the conference itself, for the simple reason that I have not the slightest recollection what these excellent men discussed during their days together. I could hazard a guess. The Lambeth Conference of Bishops might have been mentioned. The creation of a new territory for the Anglican Church somewhere in the world was bound to be an item. The truth is that, then as now, these matters failed to grip my attention and they have happily faded from memory.

There is one event that remains clear, however, and that is our afternoon visit to the White House. For some extraordinary reason, many Archbishops and Bishops seem to enjoy travelling together. Perhaps they feel there is safety in numbers, or perhaps it is simply that the flock instinct comes naturally to shepherds. If nothing else, of course, a Bishop is less likely to get lost if there is someone with him to check the tickets.

I am reminded of one young man who lived in Washington and invited his elderly aunt in England to visit him. He told her that she was to buy a ticket that deposited her at Dulles International airport, where he would meet her. 'Phone me when you get to the airport,' he said casually. He was somewhat taken aback when his aunt did phone him. She said he was not to worry about collecting her. She would take a taxi. 'Where exactly are you?' he queried. 'Dallas, of course,' she replied. Bishops have similarly unworldly tendencies, believe me.

On the day of the visit to the White House, the Chaplain and I boarded the coach along with the Revd Sam and several dozen Archbishops. Had there been an accident, the whole Anglican Communion might be very different today. There was no trouble, however, and we arrived safely. The White House security staff, although expecting this divine gathering, were nevertheless a little startled at the sight of so much purple. The clerics had donned their best garments for the visit. We were ushered cautiously through the gates. There was a slight disappointment, as the President had recently been shot. Not fatally, I am glad to say, but the injuries he sustained were sufficient to ensure that he remained in California, leaving the running of the shop to his deputy.

The party was greeted at the main door by a senior official wearing a very sharp suit and an equally incisive smile. The Archbishop, the Chaplain and myself were ushered to one side for a private conversation with the Vice President (as I have mentioned previously, Canterbury, although equal with other Archbishops, was head boy and thus received occasional treats) while the others were taken on a guided tour of this rather small but interesting building. Official secrets being what they are, I am obliged to pass over the details of that private conversation, although I can reveal that the meeting was cordial and that gifts were exchanged.

The Chaplain and I were in charge of the Archbishop's gifts, and a great nuisance they were too. Prior to any visit abroad, two large cases were stocked with a variety of trinkets. There were glass goblets engraved with a picture of Canterbury Cathedral, tiny enamel pillboxes bearing a coloured picture of Lambeth Palace, numerous signed photographs of His Grace decked out in his best Sunday kit, religious medallions – in fact, all the sort of stuff that has been the stock in trade of religious leaders across the generations. In return for these knick-knacks, we accumulated the most remarkable collection of paraphernalia you can possibly imagine. It was always a puzzle to know what to do with the stuff once it was back in Lambeth Palace, but more about that later.

We had naturally brought with us a most suitable gift for the White House. I know readers will find this all very unsatisfactory, but once again I have completely forgotten what it was. It was certainly a superior gift and not a coloured tea towel or some other such trifle. I can say that with confidence, as we would certainly have wanted our esteem for the President of the United States to be reflected in the gift we were to offer. Before our departure from the White House, it (whatever it was) was duly handed over. The grateful recipient expressed much pleasure and beckoned to an aide, with whom he had a whispered conversation. The aide left the room and returned a moment or so later bearing an extremely handsome box.

'The President is so very sorry not to be here today,' said our acting host. (As he had recently been shot and wounded, we felt the President had a respectable excuse.) 'But before you leave he would like you to have this personal gift, Archbishop.'

He handed the box over and, like a participant in a quiz show, the Archbishop was encouraged to open it there and then. He did so and it was his turn to express extreme pleasure as he pulled a glass jar from the box.

'You will have seen that the President has an identical jar on his desk in the Oval Office,' said the Vice President. 'He keeps jellybeans in it.'

The Archbishop blinked. He had not seen jellybeans since he was a boy in Liverpool. The jar was returned to its box and handed across to the Chaplain for safekeeping. The Chaplain, a diplomat of the highest order, remained impassive throughout this moving exchange of valuables. Only those who knew him well would have been aware of his private thoughts about the priceless object.

Farewells were said, sentiments of goodwill were exchanged, and we were reunited with our band of purple-clad brothers. The Chaplain remained unusually silent during the journey back to our lodgings.

A week later, safely back within the walls of Lambeth Palace, we unpacked the gifts amassed during the Archbishop's American tour. The usual collection of diocesan shields, engraved scrolls and coffee mugs made their appearance. 'By the way,' I said. 'Where's the famous jellybean jar?'

The Chaplain did not reply immediately. When he did, it was in a cheerful manner. 'You didn't hear, my dear Terry?' he said. 'Most regrettably, it was smashed on the journey home. The box proved to be insufficiently strong to protect it. A great shame.'

I said no more and resumed the unpacking. I shared the Chaplain's distress. It was indeed a most unfortunate accident.

5

A Private Dinner at The Ritz

It was a certain Mr Ward McAllister who once remarked that there are only about 400 people in New York society. I know nothing about Mr McAllister, except that he departed this life in 1895 and is reported to have made that portentous statement in the *New York Tribune*. Since his assertion appeared in a newspaper, there can be no doubt whatsoever as to its veracity. Those whose knowledge of the Americas is not based on frequent visits and intimate friendships might well be forgiven for imagining that the USA is a land of democratic equality. It is a sad mistake to do so. Take New York, for example. Even today, that great metropolis continues to be dominated by a wealthy elite. They number exactly 400. How do I know? Well, I've met them, every single one.

Mr Ward McAllister must surely have known the New York elite, and therefore must certainly have stumbled across members of the Episcopal Church. I am aware that times are changing and the Episcopal Church is not what it was. Be that as it may, even though the great and the good have been leaving it in droves, they continue to retain an affection for the Church that nourished them in their youth and sustained their forebears. When they heard that the Archbishop of Canterbury was in town, recollections of the past flashed before their eyes, as though the last trump was about to be blown. In short, they wanted to meet him.

The Archbishop had a full programme in New York. In order to ensure that there was a little money in the Lambeth Palace Garden Fund, he was obliged to make a pilgrimage to Trinity Church Wall Street. A casual visitor might imagine that this tiny edifice would be totally dominated by the massive skyscrapers surrounding it. As students of the Bible will be aware, however, it is man that looketh on the outward appearance. A more diligent observer will ask to look at the books. In the case of Trinity Church, even the shortest inspection of the records will reveal that the tower blocks for as far as the eye can see are owned by the parish. Any Archbishop with a concern for Lambeth horticulture would be foolish not to spend at least an hour amidst such fruitful glass and concrete.

On the way back to 815, a slight diversion occurred. The Archbishop had to pass the Town Hall and it would have been churlish not to call in for a cup of tea with the Mayor.

No matter who occupies the office of Mayor in New York, one can guarantee that when a visiting dignitary enters the humble parlour of this great man he will be in for a bruising half hour of raw politics. This is all the Mayor of New York knows. Politics gets him out of bed in the morning and tucks him up at night. He has politics with his pastrami sandwich at lunchtime and another liberal portion with his first dry martini of the evening. When he drives through New York and looks out on Trinity Wall Street, what does he see? Politics. When he hears that the Archbishop of Canterbury is in town, what does he think? Politics. When he meets the Archbishop, what does he talk about? I shall leave you to guess, but I can assure you that the Lambeth Palace flowerbeds were not on the agenda.

After listening to the Mayor for a solid half hour, the Archbishop tottered back to his car for yet another hurried journey through the metropolis. This may be one of the most secular cities in the world, but the Archbishop's programme was stuffed full of ritual visits. Harlem had to be on the programme. Where in Harlem? Where else but a black church, with a social outreach programme and a clergyman who talked nothing but religion and politics. The cleric was very large and his face shone with a holy political glow.

Unlike dear old Trinity, the church in Harlem dominated simply because it was the only building in a good state of repair. It was surrounded by buildings that looked as though they had been burned out several times and then used for practice by the local fire brigade. The people in the church were very jolly and welcoming, however, and the Archbishop was very jolly with them in return.

Then it was back into the car and off once again to the next engagement. I trust you are getting the picture. In New York there was not a minute to spare. Every waking moment was taken up with visits. Still to come were the cathedral and another ritual visit, this time to the Cardinal. It was all very hectic – and political.

A long time before the Archbishop's visit, when we were making the initial preparations for the New York programme, it became clear that *everyone* wanted in on the act. That is not at all unusual, but in New York those who want in know how to get in. If they are left out, someone is liable to get hurt. A certain clergyman in New York definitely wanted to be included in the programme. Not for his own sake of course, certainly not: his sole motive in requesting a place in the running order was because he ministered to the famous 400 of the city.

'We must entertain the Archbishop,' he said when he visited me some months before the visit. 'We always entertain an Archbishop of Canterbury when he comes to town. Usually we go to The Ritz Carlton or some other such place. It's very nice.'

I believed him. A discreet dinner with a few fine wines would be most acceptable to all but the incurably miserable. Try as I might, however, the programme was so political that there was not even the smallest space for a gourmet evening. To his great disappointment, I had to say no.

'I'll tell you what,' he said, just as we were preparing to say farewell. 'The Archbishop has to eat, doesn't he?'

I agreed with him. Although I had heard of saints of the Church managing to survive on nothing more than the Communion host for 40 years, His Grace of Canterbury had not achieved that degree of sanctity and was known to have a modest hot dinner now and again.

'What if I lay on a private dinner at The Ritz? Private, I assure you. The Archbishop can come in, eat and leave. Totally relaxed. Totally private.'

'Are you sure that won't take long?' I queried.

'Not at all,' he replied. 'In – eat – out.'

The deal was struck. Instead of repairing to our air-conditioned lodgings on 815 to enjoy the only private space in our programme, we would glide into The Ritz Carlton for what I hoped would be a refreshing and peaceful evening meal, courtesy of our clerical host.

We did the cathedral and conversed with the Cardinal. Afterwards the British Consul had arranged something or other, but by now everything was so political that we were dizzy and my recollections of the rest of that afternoon are hazy at best.

The cocktail hour eventually arrived and our car made its way through the evening traffic. 'Phew,' said His Grace. 'What a day. What next?'

'That's it,' I said cheerfully. 'We now go for a quiet dinner. A room has been arranged for you to rest in for a moment, and then we go down for a private meal. No speeches. Nothing.'

The Archbishop was gratified and, one likes to think, silently congratulating himself on having appointed such an expert planner who would ensure that the programme, although full, left enough time for that degree of quiet so necessary to maintain health and wholeness.

We arrived at the hotel. Our clerical host stood on the steps. 'Good evening, Your Grace. This way, please.'

I moved alongside. 'Are we going to the room?' I queried.

He gave me an impatient look. 'Room?' he repeated. 'We're going to the Ballroom, if that's what you mean.'

That was not what I meant, and he knew it. Before I could reply, half a dozen photographers leapt from the shadows and began to blind everyone in sight. We swept onwards.

'What *is* going on?' I muttered as we swept. The cleric ignored me. In the distance I could hear the sound of an orchestra. As we approached some heavy gilt doors, they swung open and we were propelled into a grand room – full of the famous 400. They all stood in line like affluent pensioners in a Post Office queue.

'Come, Archbishop,' said the cleric. 'If you stand at the front I shall introduce you to each in turn, after which we can all have a drink and go down to dinner. I shall say a few words of welcome, and you will be able to speak at the end of the meal.'

The Archbishop shot me a look of agonized despair and moved helplessly towards the podium. There was nothing I could do.

'Look,' I said afterwards when I was alone with the cleric. 'You told me this was to be a *private* dinner.'

'But it was, Mr Waite,' he stuttered. 'Everyone was privately invited.'

There was no answer to that. I said goodbye, turned away and thought for a moment. Politics, I thought. Damn politics. That's all this city knows.

* * * * *

I have had long experience of the airlines of this world. I have flown in Tiger Moths and Comets and on Concorde. I have met, and privately evaluated, the cabin staff of our times. I have been sympathetic to their trials – often they are called to deal with passengers who are highly nervous and somewhat fractious in their behaviour. I have, in short, the greatest admiration for airline staff – with some notable exceptions.

Although the famous 400 in New York knew without a shadow of a doubt who the Archbishop of Canterbury was, not all the citizens of this great political democracy were familiar with the successor of St Augustine. Why should they be? Dissenters left our shores determined to make a new life for themselves and forget their unhappy past. Why should American airline staff be exceptional in this respect? Every day some religious leader or other would be sipping a cocktail in the comfort of the first-class cabin and claiming to have the answer to life's thorniest problems. So what? Canterbury? Where's that?

His Grace presented himself at JFK Airport, bound for California. On arrival at the terminal, we encountered some confusion. Whilst the airline staff were clearly impressed by the cavalcade of cars that pulled up outside the terminal building and took a fancy to the purple cassock that the Archbishop was wearing, they had no idea who he was. Expecting otherwise, I presented our tickets without further explanation.

Now, if you imagine for one moment that America is the land of efficiency, then you are likely to be disillusioned. It is not. They may have computers. They may have every device under the sun for checking this, that and the other thing. Whether they have efficiency, however, is questionable to say the least.

'Where to?' said the girl behind the counter as I handed over the tickets.

'Is there a VIP lounge?' I enquired.

'No,' she replied.

'Is there a lounge?'

'No.'

It dawned on me that I was possibly dealing with a certain level of ignorance here. 'This is the Archbishop of Canterbury and we are travelling to California.'

The girl looked at the Archbishop as though he was a fugitive from justice. 'Tickets,' she demanded.

By now other members of the party had entered the departure area and we were forming quite an impressive group. 'Are you all travelling?' she asked.

We assured her that only three people were booked onto the flight to Los Angeles. The remainder were well-wishers, augmented by members of the group of 400, who were here for political reasons.

'Is that the Lord?' she queried when she examined His Grace's passport and recognized him from the photograph.

'Well, not quite,' I responded, 'but he does rank after the royal family in England.' I hoped that this pompous reference might help speed us on our way.

The girl took a closer look at Dr Runcie, who was engaged in a conversation about air-conditioning with the PB. 'I've never met a Lord,' she said.

'Meet one now,' I answered and introduced His Grace to the lady.

'Good afternoon, Your Worship,' she said. 'I'm sorry, but

the VIP lounge has yet to be finished. There was a leak.' Dr
Runcie nodded, not quite understanding what she was talking
about. I wondered if he was sharing my momentary but vivid
recollection of that rainswept night during our Scottish travels.

I interrupted hastily, realizing that it is quite common for
individuals to become totally confused and lose all track of
conversation when confronted with presidents, lords, or others
with ornamental designations. 'We're travelling to California,' I
said, 'where we're to be met by a reception party. Perhaps you
might cable ahead to let them know we're on our way?'

She nodded and took our tickets. 'We don't have a VIP
lounge at the moment,' she said once more, 'but I can put you
in the Manager's office. Follow me.'

We obeyed, and began the obligatory march through the
building. The Manager's office was hardly a haven of tranquillity. Several fax machines poured out reams of paper. TV
screens flickered. Large paper cups littered overcrowded desks.
It appeared that the Manager shared his office with at least half
a dozen others, all with a casual approach to order.

No sooner had we settled into a corner and been handed
some gigantic receptacles full of what they called 'coffee' than
the door flew open and our hostess appeared with a sheaf of
tickets in her hand. 'Quick!' she gasped. 'Your plane is about
to depart!'

I looked at my watch. Surely, I thought, it's not yet time.
Trusting soul that I am, however, I took the documents from
her and we all set off at a brisk pace for the aeroplane.

The journey was uneventful and we prepared ourselves
for the official reception at LA Airport. Our papers told us that

the Mayor of the city was to be there, along with the Bishop, the British Consul and the many others who had also got in on the act.

We touched down. I looked through the window and suddenly felt nervous. It hardly looked like LA Airport to me. I remembered the occasion when the late John Betjeman arrived by train at the English rural town of Diss. 'Well,' he said, 'we've arrived at a station, but where is Diss?'

I turned to the air hostess. 'This is California, isn't it?' I asked.

She gave me a reassuring smile. 'Sure is.'

Somewhat relieved, we stepped from the plane into the warm sunlight. The only person in sight was a young lady at the foot of the steps. 'Perhaps you could tell me where the welcoming party is?' I asked, feeling increasingly apprehensive.

She looked at me as though I had just arrived from another planet. 'Who?' she said. I will not bore you with further dialogue, as it was desultory. We followed her suggestion and went across to the main building.

The Chaplain touched my elbow. 'By the way,' he whispered, 'were we supposed to arrive in downtown Burbank?' He pointed towards a sign above the entrance to the terminal building.

I opened the briefing file and scanned the notes. We were certainly not supposed to arrive in Burbank. We were supposed to arrive in the main terminal at LA International Airport.

This was a genuine emergency. Within a few moments we were surrounded by the uncomfortable chaos of yet another

Manager's office. Telephones rang incessantly. The Archbishop looked puzzled. The Chaplain scribbled. I moved from one telephone to another. Finally, contact was made with LA, some few miles away. There, I was told, a large welcoming party was awaiting us. Our plane had arrived, and the Mayor had found himself greeting personally a couple of hundred startled New Yorkers, who greatly appreciated this spontaneous political gesture. He had become alarmed when there appeared to be no Archbishop on board, particularly when it was confirmed that Dr Runcie and his party had boarded a flight to LA. It was some relief, therefore, when he discovered exactly where we were.

'Stay there!' shouted an aide over the phone. 'The Mayor and his party will be over soon.' Indeed they were. We were still sipping from the obligatory paper cups when we heard the familiar sound of police sirens as our official greeters pulled up on the tarmac.

What a glorious muddle. No one had spotted or challenged the fact that we had been put on the wrong aircraft. This most fundamental point had certainly passed me by, but surely the airline staff should notice these things?

'The United States,' said the Chaplain, as we relaxed some days later at the Bishop's home on Sunset Boulevard, 'is not quite as efficient as I expected. Do you recollect Mark Twain's words on the subject?' I waited for the wisdom. 'He said that America requires distance to give it its highest charm. We return home tomorrow. I'm sure we shall appreciate it enormously.'

6

The Archmobile

The Archbishop was a good traveller. He needed to be. Not only did he have to travel throughout the world, he frequently had to travel between Lambeth Palace and his other home in Canterbury. The fact that since the twelfth century Archbishops have resided in London and not in the famed city of Canterbury is due in part to one of those tedious disputes that are the very stuff of history. Not surprisingly, it had to do with power.

Since the time of Augustine, Archbishops had chosen to exercise their metropolitical authority from this modest Kentish city. Alas, all was not tranquil in Canterbury and several Archbishops found themselves living next door to the ecclesiastical equivalent of neighbours from hell. Perhaps that is rather a harsh way to describe the monks of the Priory of Christ Church, but across the years they succeeded in irritating more than one Archbishop. At the time of the Norman Conquest, one writer tells us that intellectually the monks were scarcely up to the mark. He records that they had more than their fair share of gold and silver, were very fond of their horses, dogs and hawks, and kept a table that hardly reflected the frugality of their religious calling.

Archbishop Lanfranc did his best to get the monks to edge a little closer to the Rule of St Benedict and to some extent succeeded, but later Archbishops lost their grip on the brothers and relationships deteriorated yet again. Put simply, the monks wanted control over the election of Archbishops and most, if not all, of the Archbishops wanted none of that.

It was Archbishop Baldwin who finally decided that enough was enough, and he determined to found a collegiate church at nearby Hackington. Here, just a short distance from the troublesome Christ Church, it was planned that the Archbishop would be surrounded by his personal staff and even the King himself would have a prebendal stall. When the monks voiced their protest at the erosion of their powers, they were thrown into prison.

To cut a long and troublesome story short, eventually a compromise was reached. The Hackington project was suspended and transferred to Lambeth in London. Although the college never materialized on the bank of the Thames, the site did become the main residence for Archbishops of Canterbury and is so to this day.

It was an ideal site, not least because the court itself had moved from Winchester to Westminster, just over the river from Lambeth, and at that time the Primate was well in favour with the King. Poor Archbishop Baldwin did not live to enjoy life by the Thames, however. He died in the Holy Land in 1190, just one year after Henry II passed away. It was about then that building work started on the site of the old royal manor at Lambeth under the able supervision of Archbishop Hubert Walter.

That, dear reader, is the story of how all Archbishops since that day have come to commute between Kent and London. It could be argued that the story is infinitely more complicated than I have made it seem. History, however, is open to a variety of interpretations, and I rather like the above version.

Archbishop Runcie was certainly an accomplished traveller, as I have said. He was modest in his eating and drinking habits, and quite able to endure the recycled atmosphere of a jumbo jet and still emerge to greet a welcoming party on the other side of the world as though he had just completed a relaxing Mediterranean cruise. He once assured me that, in his humble opinion, the majority of long-distance travellers were not suffering from jet lag. Rather, he believed, they were the victims of alcoholic poisoning. As a lifelong airline traveller, I am inclined to believe him.

Without fail, wherever we went our hosts were most anxious to please. On one occasion, sometime in the mid-eighties, we visited Canada. I do not know why it is, but many people who ought to know better have been quite rude about Canada.

'A few acres of snow,' said Voltaire dismissively. Al Capone claimed that he did not even know what street Canada was on. What on earth Gibbon meant when he wrote that modern Canada was an exact picture of ancient Germany, I cannot imagine. I think we might settle more happily for the words of the great Winston Churchill, who put all the above in their place when he told the world that Canada was the linchpin of the English-speaking world. I hesitate to guess what the French thought about that, but Churchill undoubtedly knew that one cannot please all of the people all of the time, and no doubt intended to throw the French a good word or two in the future, if they behaved themselves.

Until we arrived there, I was unaware that Canada got its name from two Spanish words, *aca* and *nada*, said to mean 'there is nothing here'. This proved to be incorrect as far as I could see, and once again is typical of the burden Canadians have had to suffer. We saw plenty there. We dined with the Prime Minister, took tea with the Governor General, and met numerous inhabitants of the forests, mountains and plains of that great country.

The second week of the tour found us in some rural back-water, the name of which escapes me. It might have been Grandpappy Canyon, or Lonnigans Reach, but no matter – the name is of no consequence. The good citizens of this delight-ful retreat were overwhelmed by our visit. They had hardly seen a clergyman before, let alone an Archbishop of Canterbury. They were, however, keen watchers of television and they had followed His Holiness the Pope as he travelled in true pontifical style across the globe. No doubt they wished that His Holiness might have spent an hour or so in their company, but heaven had given them a different blessing and they had His Grace of Canterbury instead. They were determined to show what they could do.

They had noticed that the Holy Father frequently travelled across terra firma in a Popemobile. This was a luxury car with a transparent, bullet-proof dome, beneath which the Pope might stand and bless the multitudes. Popemobiles were not in regular production in Canada and the importation of one would have decimated the municipal budget for generations to come. Nonetheless, the loyal Anglicans of Canada were not to be outdone.

The Archbishop's programme for his visit to this devout corner of the Anglican Communion was full, as ever. The curious of the town (of whom there were many) were anxious to catch sight of His Grace. The church was too small to admit everyone. The solution to this problem? Let the Archbishop and his Chaplain travel through the streets in an Archmobile.

On the morning of the visit we drove to the local vicarage. As the Vicar briefed us on the programme for the day, I glanced through the study window and noticed a curious-looking vehicle in the front drive. Closer inspection revealed that it was a pickup truck belonging to a local garage. It was hard to overlook this latter fact, as the name of the garage was blazoned across the side of the vehicle. In the front seat sat a stout gentleman wearing a 10-gallon hat and chewing a large cigar. On the back there was a structure that resembled a primitive greenhouse. Rough wooden posts had been lashed together, providing a frame for a tent of transparent polythene. My feelings of anxiety increased as we left the study and walked towards the mobile monstrosity.

'We were uncertain about the weather,' said the Vicar. 'So many people want to see you, Archbishop, that we decided to drive you to the church in style. We didn't want you to get wet if it rained.'

As the early morning sun was already beating down with extraordinary ferocity, there seemed little danger of a soaking. The Archbishop glanced nervously at the greenhouse and severely at me. The Vicar moved towards the pickup.

'If you and the Chaplain would ride in the back, Your Grace, Mr Waite can follow in one of the cars.' It was now the turn of the Chaplain to give me an agonized look.

Gingerly, the Archbishop and his faithful Chaplain stepped onto a little platform beneath the polythene. The driver started the engine, inserted a cassette of hymns into the tapedeck and edged forwards. I clambered into the air-conditioned bliss of my automobile and followed at a suitable distance.

'I guess it's mighty hot in there,' muttered my driver as we processed down the main street. I guessed it was also, as I could see the Chaplain mopping his brow with a large red handkerchief. Suddenly I noticed that the Chaplain had hoisted up his cassock and appeared to be rummaging through his trouser pockets. Having found what he was looking for, he began to attack the polythene for all he was worth. A large hole appeared in the side of the greenhouse and, to the delight of the faithful, the Chaplain's perspiring head emerged through it.

By now we were almost at the church. When we stopped, I leapt out of the car, ran towards the pickup and lifted the heavy plastic flap. 'Quick!' said the Chaplain as he supported his charge. 'The Archbishop is soaked. Get the robe case. He must have a change of clothes, otherwise he'll catch his death of cold.'

A limp but still genial Archbishop emerged from his private tropical hell into the warm Canadian sun and was speedily ushered into the vestry. He did get a change of clothing and remained well. The Chaplain caught a cold. I resolved to take a great deal more care about modes of transport in the future. Let it never be said that our Canadian hosts did not mean well, however. Of course they did.

Later that evening, when the Chaplain and I were enjoying an evening cup of cocoa, I referred once again to the rudeness and, indeed, the inconsistency of certain commentators about Canada. 'Do you know,' I said, 'that even the otherwise stalwart Churchill once faltered in his support? When he was flying across the country one day, he looked out of the window and is reported to have exclaimed, "Bloody country!"'

The Chaplain yawned. 'Very true, dear Terry. Very true.'

I was puzzled. Was the Chaplain referring to the content of Churchill's statement, or to the rudeness and inconsistency of which I spoke? I never found out. At that very moment he stood up, said goodnight and went to bed.

7

Questions about Bears

I remember reading about the Yukon as a child, from ancient copies of *The Boy's Own Paper*. It was portrayed as a rough, tough land where the mosquitoes were as big as rabbits and only the very fittest of the human species survived. I had occasion to check out this childhood memory during our extensive tour of the Dominion of Canada, when we journeyed along the Alaska Highway. As far as I can remember, the few inhabitants we met hardly appeared to be in the superhuman class – except for one remarkable young man. It turned out that he was not in fact a native of Alaska, but came from some suburban idyll near Chicago.

Our journey to *Boy's Own* land was planned with all the cunning of an SAS mission. We flew late at night in an aeroplane belonging to the Royal Canadian Air Force and touched down in total darkness. As we taxied along the runway, we strained our eyes for signs of life. In the distance we could see someone flashing a light and, although we did not have a clue what was going on, we assumed that our pilot understood the code. Clearly he did, for within a few moments the plane stopped and we bailed out into the blackness. We had come to a halt by that vehicle so beloved of all North Americans, the pickup truck. This was a very superior model – in fact, to be more accurate, it was not a pickup truck at all. It was what is now more commonly referred to as a 'people carrier' and I was delighted to see that there was not a single hint of polythene about its superstructure.

Given the undercover nature of our arrival, it was a slight disappointment when, instead of being greeted by a man in a woolly hat and a face covered in bootpolish, a young clergyman stepped forward to greet us. 'Good evening, Padre,' I said, determined to remain within the spirit of the adventure. 'This is Alaska, is it not?'

'Good evening, Your Grace,' he said, quite properly ignoring both me and the Chaplain. 'If you step inside, Sir, we will ensure that the luggage is loaded.'

By now, readers will know that we were not the lightest of travellers. Dozens of cases were hauled out of the hold and tossed across to the cleric, who did his best to arrange them in the back of his limo. The Archbishop wrapped his purple scarf around his neck and clambered into the front seat of the vehicle.

'Where's my black bag?' he muttered.

The famous black bag was carried by His Grace or one of his trusty assistants on every overseas mission. It was an ordinary leather briefcase, which usually contained a few of the Archbishop's handwritten notes and perhaps one or two cough pastilles. The Archbishop clung to it like a safety blanket, so much so that we informed the curious that, as the President of the USA carried a similar bag in case war should break out, so the Archbishop carried one in readiness for the unlikely event of there being a sudden outbreak of peace. The bag was handed to His Grace, who took it firmly with him into the front seat.

I assumed it was too dangerous for the RCAF to stay a moment longer than necessary, for as soon as our goods were unloaded they shot back into their cockpit and disappeared into the night. Once the plane had departed, we appreciated more fully the stillness and remoteness of our surroundings.

'We've got quite a journey ahead,' said the clerical agent. 'I'll do my best to contact someone to arrange a meal. If you had been earlier, you would have got one at Mother's Cosy Corner, but I'm afraid that won't be open now.'

A little gentle interrogation of our man revealed that Mother's Cosy Corner was the only hotel in Haines Junction and rooms had been booked for us in that establishment. The cleric also disappeared into the night, but returned after a moment or so with the news that one of his trusty parishioners was preparing a meal and everything would be in order on arrival.

The Chaplain and I squeezed ourselves between the suitcases and we drove away from the secret airstrip into the gloom. The Alaska Highway can feel awfully lonely. There are plenty of trees. They line the road for mile after mile. Between the trees, our man informed us, there are often bears – bad-tempered bears; bears that can smell food from a distance of miles.

'If you're out walking,' said the agent, 'keep food covered at all times.'

I wondered how it would be possible both to eat a sandwich and to keep it covered, but, knowing how irritated local agents can get when seemingly stupid questions are asked, I remained quiet. I also wondered when we were likely to be walking along the highway at night, but again I kept my own counsel.

'This is a very lonely part of the world,' said our man, obviously reading my mind. 'We won't see any other traffic tonight.'

He was right. We drove for mile after mile, the headlights of the vehicle fortunately picking out nothing more exciting than pine trees, until I reached that point in a long journey when one suddenly becomes aware of the tremendous weight of one's eyelids. Then I thought I saw something ahead of us. 'Good heavens!' I exclaimed. 'Is that a bear?'

The Archbishop quickly stuffed a half-eaten apple into his black bag and peered into the distance. Unconcerned, the driver drove smoothly on. 'It looks like a hitchhiker,' he said, in that casual manner so often adopted by Alaskan supermen.

'A *what*?' I responded in astonishment. By now it was clear that this was indeed a human form, and within a moment we had passed him. 'Will he get a lift?' I enquired, remembering how even baby bears were greedy enough to pinch a little girl's porridge.

'Doubtful,' said the agent. 'No traffic at this time of night.'

'We should stop,' I said. Dr Runcie, never one to leave a person by the wayside, immediately agreed. The people carrier, however, already had its full complement of both people and luggage and there was little room. 'He can squeeze in up here,' said His Grace, making room in the front.

The cleric brought the vehicle to a halt and reversed back along the highway. A young man carrying a haversack appeared by the side of the carrier. 'Where are you going?' asked the cleric.

'Anchorage,' replied the intrepid hiker. As far as I could work out, Anchorage was a very long way indeed from our present position.

'We can take you a few miles along the way,' said our trusted agent. 'Jump in.' The young man removed his rucksack and we stowed it in the back, then he clambered in beside Dr Runcie and the driver and off we went.

You can imagine how the conversation went. First the young man was questioned about bears. He said that he had not seen any, but he was aware that they were liable to jump out of the forest from time to time. Naturally we asked him what he was doing on the Alaska Highway so late at night. He was a student travelling through Canada, he told us, and was on his way to the airport to catch a flight home. He had been dropped earlier in the day at a rather inconvenient time and location, and we were the first car he had seen since his last lift several hours ago.

As he chatted, the young man noted that our driver was wearing a clerical collar. 'You're a clergyman, I see,' he remarked observantly.

Our driver admitted that he was. As Dr Runcie had his scarf tightly wound around his neck, the young man was unaware that he was in fact positioned between two clerics, one of whom was the Primate of All England. He turned round to look at the backseat passengers, and noted that the Chaplain was also in clerical costume. 'You're a clergyman also,' he said, a hint of surprise in his voice.

'I am,' said the Chaplain, 'and the gentleman next to you is the Archbishop of Canterbury.'

Our new-found friend went into a peal of merry laughter. 'Ha ha!' he cried. 'Of course! Who else would I expect to meet on the Alaska Highway at midnight?'

'Who else indeed?' replied the Chaplain.

Dr Runcie was now in a somewhat difficult position. He certainly did not want to declare that he really was the Archbishop, as this may have made the student feel uncomfortable. He decided to remain silent.

'You're a long way from home,' said the student merrily. 'Driving back to Canterbury, I suppose?'

There was not a great deal of conversation during the remainder of the journey. Our driver ascertained that the student had nowhere to stay and immediately said that he would make arrangements as soon as we arrived at our destination. Also, as he had not eaten for a while, the young man was to have supper with our group.

After another hour or so of pine trees, we emerged into a small town of wooden huts and little else. 'We're here,' said the driver. 'I'll drive directly to the place where we're to have supper.'

Shortly after that, we pulled up outside a small house. The doors were flung open and a small group ran towards the car. 'Welcome, Archbishop!' they cried. 'Welcome to Alaska!'

I have yet to see anyone anywhere look more surprised than the student. 'You mean you really *are* the Archbishop of Canterbury?' he exclaimed. The Archbishop nodded modestly and we processed into the warmth of the house.

That evening was also memorable for being the occasion when the Chaplain, for once in his life, was rendered speechless. We discovered that our hostess was originally from the UK and had moved with her husband to Canada some years previously. He worked with the National Parks Service, while she was no mean artist. Her paintings were well known throughout Canada. During the course of the meal, I noticed that she frequently glanced at the Chaplain with an expression of puzzled curiosity on her face. Finally she plucked up courage and spoke directly to him.

'You don't by any chance come from St Albans, do you?' she asked.

The Chaplain admitted that he did indeed come from St Albans; in fact, he had been born there.

'Did you live in Marshal's Drive?'

'Number 83,' he replied.

'Well,' said our hostess, 'I remember the sad day when you saw our dog run over outside our house. We lived just a few doors away.'

'Good heavens,' he exclaimed, 'you're Elizabeth!'

She nodded. She was indeed the childhood neighbour from St Alban's.

Later that night, when the student had gone to his lodgings and Dr Runcie had retired, I sat with the Chaplain before the fire. We mused together on the events of the day – the meeting of childhood friends, the Alaska Highway and the lone hitchhiker. Just before we retired, the Chaplain turned to me. 'Do you remember what the Canon Sydney Smith said?' he asked.

'Tell me,' I replied.

'He said he only had one illusion left, and that was the Archbishop of Canterbury. Alas, we have deprived that young man even of that. Good night.'

8

Dining Down Under

Of all the wits produced by the Church of England across the generations, Canon Sydney Smith ranks highly. Although the remarkable Canon of St Paul's died as long ago as 1845, his humour lingers on. Few escaped his barbs. For example, the literary Macaulay was, according to Sydney, 'like a book in breeches'. The Canon continued, in admirably ambiguous fashion, 'Macaulay has occasional flashes of silence, that make his conversation perfectly delightful.'

Apart from being a bookish man, the Canon was no mean cook. From time to time he suggested a recipe or two and, of course, he enjoyed a good meal. As he himself said:

Serenely full, the epicure would say,
Fate cannot harm me, I have dined today.

The following story will illustrate just how right Canon Smith was.

It was a dull afternoon in October. A cold wind blew across the courtyard of Lambeth Palace, scattering leaves and reminding us all that winter was about to seize us in its icy grip. I gazed forlornly at the pile of unanswered mail on my desk. Two excellent typists slaved from dawn to dusk in a vain attempt to reduce the mountain of paper, but no sooner had they dispatched one sackful than another appeared.

Each evening one of the Lambeth staff would collect the huge bundles and make his way down the long corridor. He would nod respectfully in the direction of the portraits of former Archbishops that lined the walls. He would then pass through the draughty Guard Room, still adorned with the pikestaffs of Cromwell's not so merry men, and enter the little Post Room just behind the Archbishop's private chapel.

The Post Room is positioned directly above the Lambeth Palace Road and overlooks the River Thames and the Palace of Westminster. Within it, not surprisingly, there was a postbox. The unusual thing about this particular box was that mail was introduced into it from within the Palace and dropped downwards to street level. It frequently had to be helped on its way with a long pole kept conveniently to hand. Down at street level there was a plain box, which from the outside gave no indication whatsoever of its purpose, for the absence of a slot made it impossible for passers-by to post mail into it. Postmen had to be apprised of the fact that there was indeed a box in the wall that they must take care to empty daily.

It is said that once, when a new postman took over the round, no one remembered to brief him about the secret box. Each day the Archbishop's postman tipped countless envelopes into the box and duly prodded them down with the stick, until one day he discovered that within the chute there were about 10 feet of uncollected letters. It hardly seemed to make much difference to the functioning of the Church of England, and caused many to question whether so much letter-writing was absolutely necessary.

I digress, however. Between the piles of unanswered mail on my desk lay a couple of briefing books that my secretary had finally assembled. They were marked grandly, 'First – New Zealand' and 'Second – Australia'.

Those untutored in ecclesiastical diplomacy but conversant with world geography might well wonder why New Zealand, a smaller country than Australia and, indeed, further from the United Kingdom, should come before the great land of beer and sandy beaches. The answer is simple. As far as the Anglican Communion went, New Zealand was the end of the line. Those who lived there, of course, argued on the contrary. They came at the beginning. One could argue this back and forth for ever without reaching any conclusion at all. The fact of the matter was that, whenever an Archbishop of Canterbury visited the Antipodes, he always gave a major part of his time to Australia and tacked poor old New Zealand onto the end. This infuriated the Kiwis. An Archbishop would spend days on end preaching to all and sundry across the mighty wastes of

Australia, then, just as he was on his last legs, he would have to jump on an aeroplane and be cheerful to the New Zealanders.

When Dr Runcie assumed office, several serious requests were made to me from those far-flung islands that when the Archbishop visited them he should be fresh and alert, and this meant nothing less than going there first. I readily agreed and set about preparing for the event.

It is always instructive when making such preparations to take account of the impressions of earlier visitors. I remembered that Darwin had voyaged there in HMS *Beagle* and so I took a look at what he had to say. It was not promising. He was glad to leave the place. He found a notable absence of charming simplicity among the natives and, to cap it all, said that the English he met were the very refuse of society. He concluded by saying that he did not find the country very attractive, although the one bright spot was Waimate, 'with its Christian inhabitants'. As we were visiting the Anglicans, who presumably were Christians, this latter statement gave me a crumb of comfort.

I decided to leave Darwin's comments out of the briefing papers and had a scout around for something more cheerful. It was Viscount Northcliffe who gave us something to look forward to. 'New Zealand!' he exclaimed. 'I've never seen so much to eat as I saw in New Zealand. Meat! Meat! Meat! Tea! Tea! Tea!' Well, at least that was something. I could only hope that the Archbishop would be hungry when he arrived on those sunny shores.

Preparations were duly made and one blustery autumnal morning the Archbishop, the Chaplain and I departed from the

Palace for Heathrow, driven as always by John Brown. My memory of the journey itself has faded. I believe we travelled via Los Angeles, but frankly I forget. In those days I found pleasure in travelling by air for the simple reason that for several hours one could be away from the heat and burden of life and rest a little. Travelling to New Zealand meant that for something like 24 hours there would be no telephones, no visitors and hopefully only a little work to do on the briefing papers.

Those who travel abroad in order to enjoy scenery different from that which they view from their back door might do well to heed the comments of Anthony Trollope. He said that one of the great drawbacks of travelling so many miles to New Zealand is that on arrival one has the impression that one has not succeeded in getting away from England. 'When you have arrived, there you are, as it were, next door to your own house.' His remark, made in 1873, still holds good. One could feel immediately at home in Wellington. As in London, the developers, along with the huge cranes and other tools of the demolition trade, had arrived and were busy knocking the place down.

We did not spend too long in Wellington. We visited the Beehive, as the Parliament building is called, and were treated to dinner by the Prime Minister. It was not a very memorable evening. I had the misfortune to be seated next to the chief of the New Zealand Security Service, who looked miserable and hardly uttered a word throughout the meal. In fact, our most memorable encounter in the city was not with New Zealanders at all, but with other visitors to the South Seas.

At that time, when I was not at my desk in Lambeth grappling with sackloads of mail, I was preparing for His Grace to be the first Archbishop of Canterbury to visit China. It so happened that our own brief visit to Wellington overlapped with a visit being made by the Prime Minister and Foreign Minister of that great country. What better, I thought, than to have an initial meeting with these two gentlemen in this distant outpost of Empire?

Approaches were made, and before eight o'clock one weekday morning in Wellington, the Archbishop and I waited in our suite as arranged. There was a tap on the door and two elderly Chinese entered the room. It is curious what one remembers, looking back on such encounters. The content of our discussion that day has totally gone from my memory, probably because it contained nothing more than polite pleasantries. I do, however, remember one thing clearly.

When I was a boy my father frequently told me that you could tell the character of a man by the shoes he wore. He used to recount a tale of a man he knew whose suit was threadbare and whose shoes were holed. 'Yet,' said my father, 'his shoes were always polished. Remember that.' I dutifully remembered those words as I gazed at the feet of our oriental visitors. The Foreign Minister was clearly a homely character: he shuffled in wearing a pair of carpet slippers. The Prime Minister, by contrast, wore a pair of glossy plastic shoes, complete with plastic imitation laces. No wonder the New Zealand Security Chief had looked so worried the previous evening. He was probably having the devil's own time attempting to work out what it all meant. Security chiefs take these little indicators even more seriously than my father did.

It seemed that the great and the good from every corner of the globe had landed in New Zealand all at once, for no sooner had we finished with China than we were whisked across town to greet our own Prince Charles and his new wife during their regal tour of the South Seas. Later that day we all dined together and enjoyed a very pleasant evening.

You may be thinking that it is taking rather a long time to get to the point of the story. All I can say in my defence is that it is necessary to remember that we are in New Zealand.

'If an English butler and an English nanny sat down to design a country, they would come up with New Zealand.' So said some anonymous wit, and the truth is that the gentleness of pace was reminiscent of an English country house – or so I thought until the time came to strike into the interior. We were briefed at this point that New Zealand was not quite the haven of peace and tranquillity that some might fondly imagine. The Maori question was the source of a modicum of internal strife.

The New Zealand Archbishop of the day was a man with a social conscience. He believed that the Maoris had been given a pretty rough deal across the years. He told us, and I have no reason to disbelieve him, that he was part Maori and that he was determined to do everything possible to see that his people enjoyed their rightful measure of justice. He went further. He told us that the Maoris were a hospitable people and would welcome the Archbishop like a long-lost brother. Not only that, but they would take him into the very heart of their camp and allow him to sleep with them. At this juncture the Chaplain and I took a step back, visions of English tabloid headlines flashing before our eyes.

'Perhaps you might explain that a little more clearly,' I suggested cautiously.

The part-Maori Archbishop informed us that it was the custom for a visiting dignitary to be welcomed to the Maori encampment with feasting and entertainment. When all was done in the great meeting hall, everyone wrapped themselves in blankets and nodded off. A special visitor was expected to join them as a sign of friendship and acceptance.

I have to say that I had my reservations. Images from World War II formed in my head – of exhausted Londoners bringing blankets and deckchairs onto the platforms of the London Tube during the Blitz, then spending a restless night with a thermos and several hundred wailing children. I was none too anxious to share in such an experience, and I was certainly apprehensive about Archbishop Runcie spending a night on a camping stool.

The Archbishop of New Zealand was adamant. To refuse this offer of hospitality would be to insult the Maori people, who had been insulted enough in the past by the top nobs of the Empire. Not only that, but it might well be the spark that would fuel another round of civil unrest and he would not want the Church to be responsible for that.

There was nothing for it but to comply. In preparation for this encounter, I followed my usual custom and consulted our briefing files for useful intelligence that might equip us for the soirée ahead. There was not much to go on. I did come across a comment by a chap who said that when visiting New Zealand he brought his violin with him. He said that New Zealanders generally took a great dislike to it, but the Maoris absolutely hated it and ran away when he played. 'This,' he said, 'was a useful discovery for us all, as I often took that method of civilly driving them out of our house when we grew tired of their company.' Alas, we had brought no musical instruments with us, although I considered it might be worth slipping a fiddle into the Archbishop's travelling kit in the future.

The day of the visit to the Maori encampment dawned. The Archbishop was carefully briefed. When the greeting party lunged at him with spears, he was not to flinch. When they pulled the most grotesque faces, he was not to smile. When they finally rubbed noses with him, he was not to sneeze.

As usual he followed his instructions to the letter. On our arrival at the camp, there was much dancing and general excitement. Spears were produced, faces were pulled and noses were rubbed. In no time we settled down, along with a considerable number of invited guests, for a little entertainment. It soon became clear that we were in for the sort of evening so beloved by the British Council, when stringed instruments were strummed and gentle melodies sung. In anticipation of this, we took our seats and made ourselves comfortable.

Our Maori brothers and sisters, however, had apparently been taking instruction in the art of confrontational politics. We discovered later that American instructors had visited the country and had convinced them that the only way to get true justice was to face the white invader with the evil of his ways, and to do so at every opportunity. Happily ignorant of this, we looked on as a very large Maori with an alarming hairstyle took to the stage. Instead of producing a banjo, he began to harangue the audience. It is unnecessary to dwell upon the content of his speech. Suffice to say that it dealt with exploitation, the white man and land. After about half an hour of impassioned rhetoric, he paused for breath and the audience also breathed a collective sigh of relief. Now, we thought, perhaps we would have a little singing and dancing. Alas, the American activists had been nothing if not thorough.

'Now,' said the compère, 'we will stage a role play.' And stage a role play they did. Some white chap mimed landing in New Zealand and in no time at all he was giving the locals one hell of a time. That was about it.

Then it was the turn of the compère again. He returned to the stage to help us rectify in real life the appalling situation we had witnessed in the role play. It boiled down to the handing over of much of the land, and a sizeable quantity of cash into the bargain.

When the speech came to an end, there was a little courteous applause and polite coughing. Now I understood what was really weighing on the Security Chief's mind. It was not the Chinese at all. He was worried about his apple orchards in the heart of Maori territory.

The compère approached us. 'Did you enjoy that?' he asked. It was difficult to know what to say. One could perhaps have asked him a series of penetrating questions about settlement and tenure and so on, but this was not an occasion for dialogue. In fact, he did not require an answer. Without waiting for us to speak, he instructed us to follow him into the inner sanctum, where we were to spend the night.

I could not help feeling that this was all a bit of an anticlimax. We entered the great hall and it was indeed packed full of people, but, contrary to what we had been told, the Archbishop did not have to bed down with a roomful of strangers. He was led down a corridor and ushered into a private room. And that was that.

* * * * *

Mark Twain is always good for a quote. When visiting Dunedin in the south of New Zealand, he said, 'The people are Scotch. They stopped here on their way from home to heaven – thinking they had arrived.'

Well, I can see what he was getting at. Dunedin is a fine little town. Evidence that the Scots (I think Twain was confusing the people with the drink) settled there is everywhere. The aroma of pitch-pine Presbyterianism floats through the streets. There are houses with the same curved glass windows as one sees in Edinburgh. The countryside is green and populated with grazing sheep. The sea is always blue (at least, it was when we were there). It was heavenly indeed.

It was in Dunedin that the Archbishop had an amazing encounter with none other than the great Skipper Skeggs. Skipper Skeggs, as I was told, came from a long line of fisherfolk. His ancestors had given the Maoris the slip and wisely settled as near to heaven as they could get. Admittedly, it was a bit cold and draughty in the winter, but the Skipper and his crew were a hardy lot and managed quite nicely.

Being a diligent man, and having more than a care for the community, the Skipper became Mayor of Dunedin. He assumed this high office at a time of great significance in the life of the town – namely, the opening of the new civic offices. Dunedin, having such a close affinity with that spiritual realm so often spoken of by His Grace, was naturally more than delighted to welcome him to this paradise on earth. It was surely a sign of divine favour that the first event of importance to be held in the Skipper's bright new building was a banquet in honour of the Most Revd and Rt. Hon Lord Archbishop of Canterbury.

The evening of the banquet arrived. Ladies sensibly wrapped in woollen shawls and gentlemen in neatly pressed serge suits gathered in the foyer of the building to be whisked to the top floor by one of the fastest elevators in the southern hemisphere. The Skipper was on hand to greet his guests, most importantly His Grace and accompanying party. There was a brief obligatory tour of rooms smelling of distemper and varnish, and then we too were elevated to the banqueting suite. The Skipper, being a considerate and modest man, had not invited the whole population of Dunedin to dine with His Grace. Rather, he had kept the party small so that there would be opportunity for conversation and mutual enlightenment.

As we entered the room, drinks were served and for half an hour or so we mingled, as they say. Dr Runcie was very good at this sort of activity, even though he had said on more than one occasion that there was nothing more exhausting than enforced geniality. He appeared to thrive on it. When there was an appropriate lull in the conversation, the good Skipper clapped his hands and suggested that we all be seated around the long table. A waitress appeared and began to fill the wine-glasses. We sipped at the wine and conversed further. The waitress reappeared and topped up the glasses. We sipped again and entered into yet more conversation. The waitress came back once again with fresh supplies.

By this time we felt that we were doing quite well as far as the beverages were concerned. Now a little food would be welcome. I took a look at my watch. We had already spent something like two hours in the company of the Skipper and his mates and had not yet got to the fish course. Skipper Skeggs cast me a glance, stood up and proceeded towards the kitchen.

He reappeared after several moments, looking ashen. 'We'll all have another glass of wine,' he said in as hearty a fashion as he could muster. The guests, who by now were entering into the spirit of the evening, greeted this statement warmly. Dr Runcie looked across at me. His Grace, a light eater even at the greatest of banquets, was clearly finding all this something of a strain. I went over to him.

'What's going on?' he whispered. 'Is the food ever coming?'

I moved across to the Skipper. 'Is everything all right?' I enquired.

He assured me that it was, and soup was on the way. By now a number of the guests cared not a wit if they never took food again. Wine continued to flow and as it did, so the volume of sound in the room increased to deafening proportions.

It was very late when the soup finally arrived on the table. It was even later when the meat made an appearance, and as for pudding – I think we may have given that a miss. Eventually we said our fond farewells to this most congenial party and tottered towards the elevator, leaving behind us the sound of some extremely happy guests enjoying a very splendid evening.

It was some considerable time later that we discovered what had actually happened. The Skipper had needed to take in special help for his inaugural banquet in the new building. The chef he had hired was, shall we say, rather nervous at the thought of cooking for so many of the great and the good. To calm his nerves, he took a swig from the sherry bottle and then progressed to the spirits. When the time came to get started with the job in hand, the chef was somewhat indisposed. The story goes that when the able Skipper went into the kitchen he had to set to himself and hold several packets of frozen peas under the hot water tap, as well as dig dozens of prime steaks out of the freezing cabinet.

I have to say that Skipper Skeggs gave us all an evening to remember, and Canon Sydney Smith was proved to be right. Fate did not harm the Archbishop, nor did it hurt the fine old salt of a Skipper. We left the civic building serenely full and brimming with gratitude for an enchanting evening. In later years, when we sat down to dine together in Lambeth Palace, we often looked back on the evening spent in the company of Skipper Skeggs and his crew, and more than once we raised a glass to our excellent host from that little heaven we knew as Dunedin.

9
Through a Glass Darkly

In an earlier chapter I made mention of the fact that the Revd
Sam of ACC fame was desirous of holding one of his
clandestine gatherings in Nigeria. When this intelligence first
reached my ears, I confess that I was not too pleased. I could
well understand that the Revd Sam was anxious to encourage
the rapidly expanding Anglicans in Nigeria to expand even
further, and that he also wanted to show delegates from across
the globe how the Church should really be built. All that was
very understandable. Nigeria, however, was not the most convenient country in the world to travel to. At times the airport
facilities could become somewhat stretched and the roads
in Lagos had been known to seize up for hours on end.

Nevertheless, the Revd Sam was adamant. It was all very well for the ACC to meet in comfortable billets in Washington, he said, but there came a time when reality had to be faced. Nigeria had offered to host the meeting. Nigeria it was to be.

The Revd Sam arranged a full meeting of the Council. This included Bishops, clergymen and laypeople, plus our old friends the Primus of Scotland and, of course, Archbishop Timothy of Nigeria. It was, said the Revd Sam, to be held in a new government training centre a good 60 miles from the capital.

Although during my life I have had much to do with conferences of one kind or another, I confess that I have no great love for mass gatherings. Large plenary sessions can be boring in the extreme and many are the times when I have slipped away for a siesta or a quiet walk. Duty was duty, however, and the Chaplain and I duly packed the cases and prepared to face yet again the dual nightmares of Heathrow and Lagos International Airports.

On arrival we discovered that Lagos was the same old steamy, congested hell-hole that we had previously known. This may sound unfair, but I have yet to discover any redeeming features about the place whatsoever. In certain parts of the world, some of the great cathedrals provide an oasis of peace and shelter, even though they might be situated on the main street. Not even that benefit is granted in Lagos. The Anglican cathedral, a Victorian construction of no great charm, is on one of the noisiest streets in town and the preacher has to shout in order to make himself heard above the din of traffic. It was with some relief that we spent just an hour or so in town before leaving for the bush.

We discovered that the training centre was one of those inspired projects that look so impressive on the drawing board in London, but take on a slightly different complexion when transported overseas. It was situated in the midst of an arid region of Nigeria, a two- or three-hour journey from Lagos, and was built of those materials so beloved by architects of the sixties – glass and concrete. Entering the compound was rather like entering a prison. A heavy fence surrounded the property, which was guarded by several men bearing sticks and surly expressions.

Once inside, we were shown to our rooms. Every attempt had been made to transport European concepts into Africa. What had been overlooked was the fact that Nigeria could not always depend on a regular supply of mains water or electricity. It was good to have a shower in each room, but water would have made the facility more useful. These were minor problems, however, and I shall not dwell on them.

The conference got under way. At meetings of the ACC the Archbishop of Canterbury, although President of the whole show, was given a little respite and allowed to participate in many of the sessions as an ordinary delegate. This gave him a break from always having to occupy the chair and also meant that from time to time he could relax in his room while others toiled over the thorny problems facing global Anglicanism.

It was evening. Dr Runcie was sitting in his room attempting to understand the new constitution for an Anglican province somewhere in the heart of Africa. The matter had been debated throughout the afternoon and had been tedious in the extreme. I was taking a walk along the dusty road that led from the dining hall (famous for a beef stew that would challenge the strongest of teeth and stomachs) to my own quarters.

As I strolled along, greatly looking forward to leaving for home, I saw a figure running towards me. It was a young American clergyman. 'Quickly!' he spluttered. 'There's been an accident!'

I turned and followed him. We jogged in the direction of the accommodation block. 'I don't quite know what's happened,' he said between breaths. 'I've just got a call to say the Bishop of Southwark is in trouble.'

That would have been perfectly understandable had the Bishop of Southwark been Mervyn Stockwood, who was always in trouble. As it was, Bishop Stockwood had retired some years earlier and his successor, a gentle and mild-mannered man, had no reputation for mischief-making. What could he have done?

We approached the Bishop's room. A small group of Africans stood in a circle looking down at the ground. As we moved forward we could see a body on the floor and quite a lot of blood. It was the Bishop. The American clergyman, trained in first aid, leapt into action. For some extraordinary reason, the door to each room was made of a solid sheet of thick, shatterproof glass. To my amazement, I noted that the door to this room was in pieces. Huge shards of glass littered the floor. As for the Bishop, he seemed to be on the point of suffering the death of a thousand cuts.

'What happened?' I asked as the first-aider issued instructions and attempted to bind up wounds.

'I must have walked through the door,' said the Bishop gently. 'It's extraordinary. I went clean through it.'

I left the Bishop in the careful hands of the American cleric and walked along the block to Dr Runcie's room. Always diligent, he was sitting in an uncomfortable chair reading tomorrow's briefing papers.

'Hello,' he said cheerfully, glad for any distraction. 'Everything well?'

'No,' I replied. 'Ronnie Bowlby's walked through a glass door.'

Having worked with His Grace of Canterbury for many years, I knew that he was a man who had compassion for the suffering of others. I was, however, totally unprepared for his reaction to this simple, albeit surprising, statement. He went pale and stared at me as though I had just informed him that the Cardinal Archbishop of Westminster had run off with a chorus girl.

'Good heavens!' he exclaimed. 'I was only with him an hour or so ago. He looked fine.'

At first I did not quite follow his thinking, but then I realized that Dr Runcie might have thought that the Bishop had met an accident as a result of overindulgence in the local brew. 'Oh, he's quite sober,' I said reassuringly.

Dr Runcie was not listening. 'We must inform his family right away. This will all be a terrible shock…' He stood up and hurried out of the room.

To be in a country where the telephone is less reliable than the water and electricity supply can at times be a blessing. Had Dr Runcie been able to find his way across the compound to the one and only telephone, and had that telephone been working, then the family Bowlby back in England might have been in for an even nastier shock than the wounded head of their household.

I returned to the scene of the accident. By now the cleric had swathed his episcopal charge in bandages and, I presumed, was awaiting a donkey to transport him to the nearest inn. The Bishop sat calmly on a stool, sipping from a steaming mug of something or other and puzzling about how it could all have happened.

Suddenly Dr Runcie appeared through the gloom. He stared at the Bishop. 'Ronnie, is that you?'

'Hello, Bob. Silly thing to do. Can't think how it happened.'

'My goodness,' said His Grace. 'Waite told me that you were dead!'

'I said no such thing,' I protested.

'You came to my room and I distinctly heard you say that Ronnie had walked through his last door.'

'*Glass* door,' I said. 'Not last door. *Glass* door.'

Later that evening I handed the Archbishop his papers for the morrow. 'You know,' he said, 'I thought you were trying to break the news to me gently by saying that Ronnie had walked through his last door. It's always wise to speak directly, you know.'

* * * * *

Our sojourn in Nigeria was almost over. The Revd Sam and his industrious team had worked bravely to ensure that everything went smoothly. He was nothing if not organized. I would not say that he was obsessive in this respect, but it might be fair to say that he took a legitimate pride in his organizing ability. So he ought. It was faultless ... almost.

On the last day of the conference a service had been arranged in the great, noisy cathedral in Lagos. A fleet of buses and cars would transport delegates from the conference centre into the capital and back again. The Revd Sam and his team had carefully arranged everything. Everyone agreed that there could be no better person than the Revd Sam to preach the final sermon.

The great day arrived. After lunch, weary delegates dragged themselves away from a second helping of beef stew and staggered across the compound to board their coaches. The star of the show decided that he would repair to his room and go over his sermon before boarding the last vehicle into the city.

The conference had kept the Revd Sam and his team very busy indeed. Each morning they were up at the crack of dawn, and they toiled relentlessly until late at night. Back in his room, the Revd Sam glanced at his sermon notes ... and, as though anticipating the response of his congregation, his eyes began to close. Within a moment he was sound asleep.

It was only when the service was about to begin and delegates were lining up with their banners and national symbols that someone enquired as to the whereabouts of the preacher. No one had seen him since lunchtime. How the final coach left without him remains a mystery. Why no one spotted earlier that his jovial presence was missing baffled even the wisest.

A runner was sent to find a telephone. He did not return. Another runner was sent. He too went missing. A third, more senior person left and returned with the unsurprising news

117

that the phone was not working. A fourth person was dispatched and returned to say that he had found a phone that worked, but the phone at the conference centre was out of order. There was nothing for it. People in the procession were getting impatient and the rapidly expanding Anglicans from Nigeria wanted their money's worth. Someone had to step into the breach. Our trusty friend the Primus of Scotland did the honours and saved the day.

As for the Revd Sam Van Culin, well of course he was immediately forgiven, even though nearly everyone was secretly a little pleased that such a model organizer had proved to be so human after all.

'You know,' said the cleric who had ministered with such competence to the wounded Bishop of Southwark, 'from this day on he will be known as Rip Van Culin.' And so he was.

10
Paper Tigers

I never fail to be interested in the recorded observations of other travellers. The writer Peter Fleming said that Peking resembled Oxford in several ways. I have visited Peking when it was Peking and also when it was Beijing and, try as I might, I could not see what he was getting at. It seemed to my jaundiced eye that a visiting Australian businessman got it right when he said that what Beijing needed was a few good paint salesmen.

Following the cordial breakfast meeting in Wellington with the interestingly shod Prime Minister and Foreign Minister of the great Cathay, a communication was duly received at Lambeth Palace inviting the Archbishop to make an official visit to their country. As far as the Anglican Communion was concerned, China did not exist except in the form of Hong Kong. At that time, Hong Kong was an outpost of Empire and still enjoyed a year or so on its lease. The Anglican Church was alive and well in that commercial paradise but, alas, on the mainland it was no more.

It would be beyond the brief of this chapter to detail the politics of Church life in China, but roughly speaking, the Roman Catholics there were divided into two main bodies. There was the body which was recognized and approved by the State. Then there were the others who kept loyal to the Pope and lived pretty much underground. The Anglicans had joined with many of the non-RC denominations and were marshalled under what was known as the 'Three Self Movement'. When this designation was first brought to my attention, I puzzled as to its meaning. The passing of the years has dimmed my recollection of the exact definition, but it has to do with self-reliance and other positive things that released the Chinese from the grip of the foreign missionary.

The headman of the Three Self Movement was a Chinese Anglican Bishop called Bishop Ting. When I first met him in the early eighties he was long past collecting his bus pass, and at the time of writing continues alive and well somewhere in the depths of China. I have to take my hat off to this wise old man. Never have I come across one who could perform such a delicate political balancing act with such consummate skill. He did not escape criticism, of course. There was a substantial number of non-RC Christians who regarded the Three Selfers as the worst form of appeasing apostates and the old, grey-haired Bishop as a leading contender, in China at least, for the position of the Antichrist.

In going to China at the invitation of the Three Self Movement and the People's Friendship Association, Archbishop Runcie was, as they say, making a major statement. No occupant of the chair of Augustine had set foot on the Chinese mainland before, and certainly none had bestowed a blessing on the Three Selfers. His Grace was, as usual, blazing a trail.

Beijing from the air is a gloomy-looking city. The traveller arriving during the autumn or winter will look down on a pall of coal smoke that prevents one from having any view of the municipality whatsoever. Once that cloud has been penetrated and one's feet are firmly planted on Chinese soil, one rapidly discovers that even indoors, smoke continues to be a problem. The Chinese are ferocious cigarette smokers and seem to be locked in a constant battle with other purveyors of pollution to see who can cause the most nuisance.

Our landing in Beijing was enlivened by a minor incident in which the wing of our jumbo jet smashed into the landing ramp, forcing us to remain on board for an extra hour or so while the Three Selfers and People's Friends got through several more packets of Chinese Woodbines. Finally we emerged into the haze of a normal Chinese day, to be greeted by the elderly chief of the Friendship Association and his lovely young wife. The Three Selfers were out in force, led by their able General Secretary and, as is always the case, several other unidentified hangers-on.

We were ushered out of the airport into our official cars and were driven directly to a VIP compound hidden somewhere in the centre of Beijing. Here equality was thrown to the winds. Several elegant mansions were dotted around, and outside these were parked two or three official black limousines. This was nothing less than the official compound designated for heads of State and other exalted individuals.

We swept through the portals of our own elegant mansion. A young man immediately seized Dr Runcie's black bag and made off with it, thus jeopardizing the cause of world peace for several critical moments. We hurried behind him, ploughing through the deep pile of the exquisite carpets. After a minor route march we arrived at our rooms. Mine, a modest apartment that would easily have accommodated several dozen families, was draped with long velvet curtains and was heavy with the perfume of scented wood. The rooms were liberally supplied with ashtrays, boxes of cigarettes, bowls of fruit and cool drinks. It was a materialist's paradise.

We settled into our quarters, grateful for some privacy and quiet after the long journey. I stretched myself on my ample bed. Just as my eyes were closing, I heard the gentle tinkle of the telephone bell.

'Mr Waitee.'

'Yes?'

'Mr Waitee. Doctor is here for Archbishop.'

I did not reply for a moment. Only several minutes before, I had seen Dr Runcie enter his room in pursuit of the black bag. He had looked perfectly well. 'I'll be down directly,' I said after a pause.

I hoisted myself off the bed and prepared to wade my way through the carpet back to the main hall. When I opened the door, a young man in a white coat was waiting. 'This way,' he said.

The Chinese doctor was in the hall. He wore glasses, had a bald patch and appeared somewhat nervous. It emerged that this young man had been assigned by our thoughtful hosts to accompany the Archbishop throughout his tour of China. It was important, he said, for him to examine Dr Runcie as soon as possible. There would be no problem for Dr Runcie in China. He would enjoy good health and live a long life. He, the doctor, would be by the Archbishop's side day and night. The Archbishop need not fear. He, the doctor, knew all medicines – European medicine and Chinese medicine. Whatever the Archbishop needed, he, the doctor, would see that it was granted. Dr Runcie was an honoured guest and he, the doctor, was honoured to look after such an honoured guest.

What could I do but escort him forthwith to the Archbishop's room?

At this juncture I ought to mention that Dr Runcie was not one to make a great fuss about his health. Like all of us, he suffered from minor complaints from time to time, but bore them stoically. He travelled the world quite happily, eating and drinking in moderation, and certainly did not travel with medical attendants. I carried in my bag a few pills for warding off malaria, calming an upset stomach and dealing with a headache, but that was about all. I did not think that His Grace would take too kindly to the gift of a full-time medical man. I was right.

The medical man was nothing if not thorough. He began by giving the Archbishop a complete medical check and promised that he would be by the Archbishop's side at all times. For some extraordinary reason that none of us to this day has been able to fathom, he seemed to think that the Archbishop needed to be given frequent injections of confidence. Following each event at which the Archbishop appeared, the doctor was at his elbow. 'Velly good, Archbishop,' he would mutter after His Grace had delivered a few minor comments to some Friends of the Revolution. 'Velly good speech.'

After several days of this concentrated attention, the Archbishop began to flag a little. It was one thing for the poor man to have to deal with the habitual cynicism of his Chaplain and myself. To have to listen to the constant praise of the medic and then be subjected to yet another full medical check proved infinitely more gruelling.

It so happened that illness did strike the camp but, sadly for the doctor, it felled the wrong individual. In those days, when I was a comparatively young man, I ate and drank with impunity. Where Dr Runcie was careful, I was, alas, reckless.

The Chinese are very cunning when it comes to serving meals. If one makes the mistake of taking too much to eat when the first eight or nine plates are served, then one is going to face some trouble with the following 18. On my first visit to China, when I was travelling alone, I discovered a white spirit named *Mou Tie*. I thought it might make a pleasant nightcap, but it tasted so foul that I gave the bottle away after one sip. Later on I discovered that this potion was not meant to be drunk like a fine brandy. It was meant to be thrown down during the course of a Chinese meal. Taken that way, it greatly improved the meal and, incidentally, the conversation.

We had been to the Great Hall of the People for a banquet. This sounds very grand and, in its own way, it was. However, like many such places the food left something to be desired. It was rather like sitting down to a meal in the upper regions of the Albert Hall while the cooks labour away in the basement. It takes them an age to get the food onto your plate and when it arrives it is not always in prime condition, having had ample opportunity to cool off.

We sat down at a long table and listened to speech after speech. As there was nothing better to do, I took a little of the spirit. No dishes of food appeared to go with it, as the waiter was probably still trundling his trolley along the miles of corridor. My neighbour took more spirit and offered me the same. At the end of the evening I felt somewhat queasy. The night was restless and in the morning my stomach was in active rebellion, just as it had been after the seafood supper in Nigeria. Our doctor was summoned for his first real work of the tour.

'Ha!' he said, beaming with delight at the thought of dealing with a medical problem at last. 'Ha, big man. You sick, eh? Ha!' I did not care for his bedside manner, which seemed to me to be far too jovial. 'Ha, big man. Your stomach sick, eh? Ha, velly funny!'

I failed to see the funny side and wondered what had happened to his capacity for reassuring his patients. He rummaged in his bag and produced a potion which I was instructed to take. 'This good for you, big man. Ha!'

Ha, indeed. When the doctor left, I pocketed his remedy and swallowed a simple Seltzer instead.

The Chaplain provided me with the epilogue to this story. The Archbishop was sitting quietly one afternoon preparing for a taxing banquet when the doctor tapped on the door for his routine medical examination. 'Ha, Dr Luncie,' he beamed. 'Ha, Dr Luncie is well?'

The Archbishop assured the doctor he had never felt better, at least until he had been interrupted.

'Ha, velly good!' said the doctor. 'Velly, velly good. You velly strong, Archbishop. Telly Waite, he no strong. He no strong at all. He paper tiger.'

At a stroke the doctor endeared himself to His Grace. From that day on until the end of the tour there was not one further word of complaint from the Archbishop about his faithful medical supporter, and we all remained perfectly well.

* * * * *

When Fernan Mendez Pinto visited Nanking in 1542, it must have been some city: 'Two thousand temples, thirty prisons, ten thousand silk looms.' Brother Pinto was greatly impressed and wrote at some length about the wonders of the place. Today's Nanjing is not so impressive. Like most towns in China, it is smoky, busy and needing a lick or two of Australian paint. When we visited, the 130 gates and the 24,000 houses of the Mandarins had gone for ever. We did, however, find the modest home of Bishop Ting located near to the mighty River Yangtze. At that point the river is crossed by a very considerable bridge, but more about that in a moment.

I mentioned earlier that Bishop Ting was an Anglican Bishop, and the head of the interdenominational Three Self Movement. The Bishop was an important man in China. Not only was he an important religious figure, he also enjoyed a prominent position within the political structures of State. It was this latter fact that caused so many of the more fervent Christian groups to regard him with more than a degree of suspicion. His position with the government was purely advisory, of course, and he maintained his Christian stance with conviction. The secret of understanding Bishop Ting was to remember that first and foremost he was Chinese. He spoke perfect English, had many English friends, was well travelled and was no mean scholar, but above all he was Chinese. Like the bamboo, he could bend with circumstance but not snap. That was his secret.

I have already said that the Archbishop of Canterbury was the first holder of the office to visit mainland China. This also required a certain gymnastic talent. He had to keep the interests of the Church firmly to the fore and at the same time steer a course through the choppy political waters of developing China. The Archbishop could not have had a better teacher than wise old Bishop Ting. The Bishop did not believe in confrontational politics, nor did he believe in committing himself before the situation was exactly right. He would have been totally at home as a Cardinal in the Vatican.

During the course of his visit, the Archbishop was invited to attend and preach at various church services. Given that the Three Selfers were made up of former Methodists, Presbyterians, Anglicans and so on, the services tended to be of the 'hymn sandwich' variety – there would be a hymn, a prayer, another hymn, a reading, another hymn, etc. Frankly, to an outsider such as myself, they were a tad boring, but one could quite easily be cheered by the sight of so many Chinese singing familiar hymns in their own language.

Also during the course of the visit, several theological points were discussed by the Archbishop and the Bishop, and the issue of Holy Communion arose. To those unfamiliar with doctrinal debates, the following will be virtually incomprehensible. I shall be brief. The question was, should the Archbishop celebrate Holy Communion according to the Anglican rite in one of the Three Self churches? The answer arrived at was no, not yet, the time was not ripe. The next question was, should the Archbishop celebrate Holy Communion according to the Anglican rite in his hotel room, making it known that visitors could attend if they so wished? The answer to this was yes, no problem. Bishop Ting was invited to attend and we left it to him to invite whom he wished in his turn.

On the morning of the Communion, the Chaplain prepared for the celebration. It brought to mind the days when Catholics in Protestant England met together in broom cupboards or between the rafters of a country house to celebrate Mass. We waited for our visitors. The clock ticked by. At the very last moment, the door opened and in walked one of the local Chinese clergy. As there was no sign of Bishop Ting, the Archbishop started the service with just the four of us.

Later that morning Dr Runcie met Bishop Ting. 'We missed you earlier,' he said in his good-hearted way.

The Bishop gave one of his enigmatic smiles. 'Ah yes,' he said. 'I'm afraid I had to pay a pastoral call and take a basket of eggs to a widow who lives across the bridge. It is rather a long walk.' It was indeed, as the Yangtze is very wide at Nanjing.

We nodded and said no more. The Bishop had decided that the time was not ripe. He did not accept the invitation to attend the Anglican service, but he did not refuse. He simply got on with his pastoral duties in his own Chinese way, and we got on with ours.

* * * * *

Bishop Ting, as you will have gathered, was a man with healthy social instincts. As commanded by the Scriptures, he visited widows and orphans, he played his full civic part in national and local life, and from time to time he travelled abroad helping foreigners to understand the complexities of the Three Self Movement. It was hardly surprising, therefore, that before leaving Nanjing he arranged for the Archbishop to attend a tea party given by the Mayor of the city.

The Archbishop of Canterbury was also well versed in many aspects of social life. He had risen through the ranks in the Church, from a humble curate in the North-east of England to the giddy heights of the throne of Augustine. During that time he had attended hundreds of bun fights and was one of the world's leading experts on weak tea and sardine sandwiches. Name a parish in the diocese of Canterbury and the Archbishop had taken tea there. Name a diocese in the Church of England and His Grace had shared bridge rolls with its

Bishop. He had dined with the Queen, supped with the Lord Mayor of London and sat down to a hearty luncheon with His Holiness the Pope. There was not a great deal the Archbishop's staff could tell their employer about social dining.

Those unaccustomed to the convivial social whirl of the higher clergy might imagine that it is quite relaxing to move from tea party to tea party sampling the home-made cakes of the faithful. In fact it is hard work, especially if one has to enter a room designed to accommodate 100 crammed with 300 individuals, all trying to get at the fruitcake. A parish clergyman who receives a visit from his Archbishop might well have arranged the church service to perfection, but when it comes to the refreshments the whole event can go to pieces. I have seen His Grace of Canterbury almost torn limb from limb by a hungry tea party crowd anxious for cakes and a blessing. It is a tribute to the Chinese to say that when they arrange a tea party they do it in style. No unseemly milling about for them.

Bishop Ting escorted us across town to a small building that in many respects resembled the sort of church hall one might find in the British Isles. I ought to explain that our visit to China came at a time when the Chinese were just putting behind them some of the more extreme excesses of the Cultural Revolution. Much had changed, but not even Chinese tailors could sew millions of new suits in a few weeks, and so the majority of individuals continued to wear the familiar Mao suit and jaunty cap.

How I wish that clerics from the diocese of Canterbury could have been with us when we entered that hall. They would have learned so much. Instead of the teeming mass of humanity that we are all led to believe is the norm in China, dignified groups with about six people in each sat quietly around little card tables. It was somewhat like an old-fashioned whist drive, except for the presence of uniforms and the absence of cards.

The Mayor, an elderly gentleman, greeted the Archbishop and escorted him through the door into a totally silent room. 'What are we supposed to do?' I whispered to Bishop Ting.

'Go from table to table,' he replied, 'and say a few words to each.'

I repeated these instructions to the Archbishop who, despite his many gifts, had yet to master Mandarin. Saying a few words to each might turn out to be a problem. He approached the first table. 'Good afternoon,' he said politely.

'Good afternoon,' everyone replied in unison and in perfect English.

'How are you all?' enquired the guest.

'Very well, thank you,' replied the partygoers.

'I'm pleased to hear that,' said the Archbishop.

I appreciate that this conversation could hardly be called stimulating, but in fact it is the sort of conversation endured by visitors to tea parties the world over. After we had visited half the tables and enjoyed an identical exchange with the occupants of each, the Mayor directed us to our own table, where we were greeted with a pot of tea and some little cakes.

'Now there will be some entertainment,' he said.

A young lady appeared with a violin and played several Chinese melodies. When she finished there was polite applause. The Mayor then took the floor and made a short speech in his own language. We guessed that he was pleased to see the Archbishop and that he wanted the Archbishop to feel at home. He then came across to where we were sitting and we set off again to visit the remaining tables in the room.

Having taken tea, the Archbishop felt a little more talkative and thought that he might extend his conversation beyond the simple dialogue recorded above. We came to a table made up of Mao-suited men. As the Archbishop approached, they all removed their caps. His Grace began in his usual manner and then turned to one man who was totally bald. 'And how are you, sir?' he enquired.

'I'm extremely well,' the bald man responded. 'Never felt better. Tell me, Archbishop, where is Brasenose on the river these days?'

It was then that I remembered the remarks made by Peter Fleming, who said that Peking resembled Oxford. Perhaps he had confused Peking with Nanking? His Grace, an old Brasenose man himself, informed the enquirer who was head of the river and how he thought Oxford would fare in the next boat race.

We said our farewells and left the members of the tea party sitting at their card tables in total silence. The Mayor escorted us to the door.

'Thank you for a lovely afternoon,' said the Archbishop.

'It's been a pleasure,' said the Mayor in perfect Oxford English.

We climbed into our car and made for the little house by the Yangtze. As we travelled in silence, I pondered the words of the Scottish bard William McGonagall:

How wonderful are the works of God
At times among His people abroad.

How wonderful indeed, I thought, how wonderful indeed.

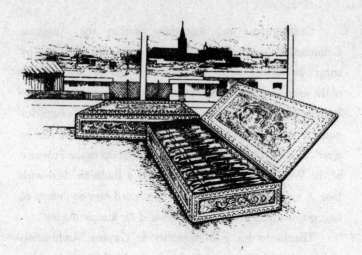

11
A Mild Despotism

At this point in my account of the Runcie years, I find myself in full sympathy with the sentiments expressed by one Lafcadio Herne, who wrote, 'I believe I am beginning to write absurdities: it is so hot that rain-clouds form in one's head.' The unfortunate Lafcadio was writing from Demerara, known today as Georgetown, the capital of Guyana. When I reflect back on the few days spent with the Archbishop and his Chaplain in that steamy corner of South America, I can still conjure up vivid pictures of 'that very fantastic and unhealthy land'. Those words were also written by Lafcadio, who clearly had a testing time in this vast, mosquito-infested sugar plantation.

Georgetown was legendary within the Anglican Communion – not because of its 'mild despotism, tempered by sugar', as Trollope wrote, but because it was the home of one of the most formidable champions of Anglicanism, Archbishop Knight. This old man ruled the West Indies from his bachelor home in Georgetown for more years than anyone could care to remember. He was the last English Archbishop in the Province of the West Indies and when he died a tradition died with him. A much younger local man succeeded him as Bishop of Georgetown, and it was he who invited Dr Runcie to visit.

Thanks to his great seniority in Guyana, Archbishop Knight was able to stand aloof from the local conflicts which were rife throughout the country. The new man, being a local boy, was not so fortunate. When we arrived he was locked in mortal conflict with his former schoolmate Forbes Burnam. Burnam was President of Guyana. That is all the history you need to know for the moment, although there is a great deal more that could be said.

Any visitor to Georgetown should make straight for the cathedral. It is a unique building, the largest wooden cathedral in the world. The largest wooden building of any kind is said to be in Wellington, New Zealand, and I have cast eyes on that structure also. There were many differences between the two, I could see, but the biggest difference was that Georgetown Cathedral was riddled with insects. At first sight it looked most impressive, but closer inspection revealed that termites and white ants had settled there when Archbishop Knight was but an infant.

The local Bishop was now faced with the problem of how to save his cathedral. He needed vast sums of cash to help persuade the termites to leave and Georgetown was hardly a wealthy place. Perhaps a UN organization might help? To enlist the help of the UN, the Bishop needed the support of the President. He was not on speaking terms with the President. Thus the termites continued with their long lunch and the future of the cathedral looked increasingly uncertain. It was Archbishop Runcie who intervened in this unhappy state of affairs.

On arrival at the airport, it was clear to us that the government of the country was not jumping up and down at the prospect of a visit by His Grace of Canterbury. The most senior representative of the British government was on hand to greet him, as was the Bishop, of course, together with several other senior clergy. There may also have been a minor information officer from the government of Guyana, but whoever it was kept such a low profile that I cannot be certain. We trundled into town with the Bishop. It was hot, that much I can remember. It was so hot and humid, in fact, that if one had been foolish enough to write notes in real ink, the ink would have smudged of its own accord.

In due course we pulled up outside the Bishop's house, formerly the residence of Archbishop Knight. 'It was a bit of a mess when we took it over,' said the Bishop sadly. 'The old man lived alone, you know, and didn't do anything to the place in 40 years. And now, just as we've got it in order, we shall have to think about the cathedral.'

During lunch, the Bishop briefed us. He had known President FB all his life. FB was the son of a prominent Methodist and claimed to be a Methodist himself, although it was many years since he had graced the portals of any church building. The fact was, FB did not like the Bishop and the Bishop did not like FB. Their mutual antipathy did not stem from their different denominational allegiances, however. The Bishop believed that FB was not the most honourable of Presidents. I shall leave it at that.

'He hasn't invited you to lunch, but he will invite you to visit him,' said the Bishop as we tucked into our papaya.

'Will you come with us?' queried the Archbishop.

The Bishop shook his head. 'That would be quite wrong. Until the President mends his ways, all the clergy will keep their distance.'

A day or so passed. We did the usual things one does on an official visit. We had lunch at the British Embassy. We made visits to schools and hospitals. We attended a cordial meeting with the local clergy. It was all very routine and all very hot. Throughout we believed that, although there was no sign of the government of the country, we were being watched very carefully and every word uttered by His Grace was being communicated verbatim to the presidential headquarters.

The days slipped by and it was almost time for us to leave this fantastic corner of the Communion. We were about to meet with the Bishop to drive out to New Amsterdam, a part of Guyana with some of the largest mosquitoes I have ever seen in my life. I am convinced that these monsters had the capacity to bore through a mosquito net with twice the power of your ordinary wood-chomping termite. Just as we were about to depart, a runner appeared with an important message. Dr Runcie was invited to the presidential home late that afternoon for a private audience with the President.

His Grace looked at the Bishop. 'Will you come with us?' he repeated, hoping for a little moral support.

The Bishop reiterated his refusal and warned the Archbishop that, once within the presidential walls, he would have to keep an eye on the clock, as FB had the habit of detaining his guests for much longer that anticipated.

That evening Dr Runcie and I settled ourselves in the back of the Bishop's car. It was dusk when we left and already quite dark when we approached the presidential compound. The whole area was powerfully illuminated and surrounded by barbed wire. It reminded me of a prison camp. We passed through security and into the inner sanctum, where we were met by a young man with the sort of haircut and dark suit that I remembered seeing in Papa Doc's Haiti. Papa Doc was known for keeping Haiti under strict control and his sinister agents were scattered liberally throughout the country. The President's aide extended some form of greeting which, as far as he was concerned, was probably extremely cordial but seemed to us to be far from welcoming.

We trudged down an antiseptic corridor lined with miniature television cameras and were shown into a small waiting room. It was all very clinical, as though we were about to meet a surgeon for a hasty consultation before being whisked off to an operating theatre.

After a few moments the door opened and we were shown into the presidential office. 'The President will be with you directly,' said the dark suit.

We slumped into a deep leather sofa and surveyed the office. It was a fairly ordinary room, apart from the fact that there were several television monitors dotted around. I assumed that there was a hidden microphone under every cushion and imagined that at that very moment FB himself was observing us from his bunker somewhere in the building.

Suddenly the door swung open and President Forbes Burnam himself entered. 'Greetings, Archbishop!' he boomed, sweeping across the room and seizing the Archbishop's hand before he could struggle up from the depths of the sofa. 'How are you, Mr Waite?' I too was struggling to get to my feet. 'Don't stand, please,' he commanded.

He left us both floundering as he moved away to sit behind his glass-topped desk. For a moment he seemed to lose interest in us as he pressed a button on a TV monitor and studied the screen carefully. Uncharitably, perhaps, I assumed he was giving his next visitors the once-over.

'Well,' he said cheerfully, turning his attention back to us. 'Good of you to come. Have a drink. Gin?'

Before we could reply, he produced from under his desk three giant tumblers and a litre bottle of gin. He poured three of the largest measures I have ever seen and handed the biggest across to the Archbishop.

'You will take some tonic with it, Archbishop?' he asked.

There was hardly room, but His Grace, a moderate drinker at all times, mumbled something about the glass being rather full and requested that the last inch of glass be topped up with tonic.

'Well,' said the President again, 'the Bishop's busy, is he? Busy man, the Bishop.' He took a swig from his glass. 'You will be staying for dinner, Archbishop, won't you? And you, Mr Waite, of course.'

This was all very unexpected. It was six-thirty, and at eight that evening the Archbishop, termites and gin permitting, had an appointment to appear in the largest wooden cathedral in the world. The Archbishop attempted to explain.

'Come now, Archbishop. This is all very unfortunate. You can't come all this way and not have dinner.'

I stepped in and explained firmly that we had understood we were coming for drinks only and that several hundred people would be waiting on the Archbishop at eight o'clock in the cathedral.

The President grinned. 'The Bishop is having some problems with that place, isn't he?'

I acknowledged that the Bishop was indeed fighting a losing battle with the insect world and needed help. FB picked up the gin bottle and waved it at the Archbishop, who politely waved it away. As FB replenished his own glass, I took the bull by the horns. I asked him if he would support an appeal to the UN to help save the building.

'Of course, Mr Waite. Delighted. Any time. Delighted. Do you smoke, Mr Waite?' Before I could answer, he snapped his fingers at one of the cameras and pressed a button on his desk. 'Gift-wrap a box of cigars for Mr Waite,' he commanded. 'And also bring one for the Archbishop.'

We looked up at one of the screens and saw a lady secretary tripping down a corridor with two parcels. There was a tap on the door, she entered and left two packets on the President's desk. 'These are excellent cigars, Archbishop,' he

141

confided. 'Fidel sends me boxes every month. Excellent cigars.'

It was just a few minutes to eight before we were able to escape the President's lair and hurry away towards the cathedral.

Not too long afterwards Forbes Burnam died. The Bishop lives on. As far as I know, the cathedral is still standing and, I believe, has been repaired. As long ago as 1859, Trollope had described the form of government in Guyana as 'a mild despotism, tempered by sugar'. If only he had substituted gin for sugar, he would have got it exactly right.

12

African Ecumenism

Frederick Cornwallis, a younger son of Charles, fourth Baron Cornwallis, was the first Primate of All England of high birth since the days of Cardinal Reginald Pole. Frederick occupied the throne of Augustine for some 15 years, from 1768 until 1783. 'In shining talents and extensive learning, other Prelates may have been superior to him,' wrote one luminary of his time. 'But in solid sense and understanding, in a right discernment of men and things, in prudence, moderation and benevolence, in affability, candour and hospitality, none of his predecessors have exceeded him.'

By any standards, that is not a bad write-up and the good, solid sense of Archbishop Frederick was demonstrated when, according to the late Mr J. Cave-Browne MA, one-time curate at St Mary, Lambeth, he abolished 'that odious distinction which had hitherto assigned to the Chaplains a lower place in the Dining-Hall, and received them as companions at his own table.'

Then, as now, the Chaplains to the Archbishop lived within the Palace walls. Indeed, they were accorded 'spacious and inviting chambers'. A minor snag was that the accommodation was situated in the Water Tower and was only accessible by a narrow, winding turret stair. Men of considerable distinction have, over the years, occupied this remote habitat at Lambeth. One has only to remember Doctors D'Oyly and Mant, who, between acting as Chaplains, laboured against the noise of the water pipes to produce their Commentary on the Bible. Being able to sit at the table of their employer, Archbishop Manners Sutton, no doubt encouraged them in their arduous task and probably also fortified them for the long climb to their humble residence.

Frederick undoubtedly demonstrated his wisdom when he moved his Chaplain a little closer to the salt at mealtimes. Being of noble birth and no doubt accustomed to being surrounded by retainers, he would recognize that a Chaplain to an Archbishop could exercise considerable influence. One who lives in the Palace, dines at the Archbishop's table, reads the Archbishop's mail (and not infrequently answers it), travels with the Archbishop, and sifts through the endless list of those who crave an audience with the Primate, enjoys a touch of power – even though at the end of the day he may have to ascend the Water Tower and resume his solitary studies.

It is now many years since an Archbishop in residence dined with his companions in hall. After a day of toil, Archbishop Runcie was wont to remove himself from his study, climb the short staircase to his modest apartment above the office and watch *The Antiques Road Show* or some other suitably instructive entertainment. Frequently, though, such modest relaxation was denied him when he was in residence at Lambeth. He might find the time to give an intimate luncheon party in the small dining room along the long corridor, or from time to time entertain on a grander scale in the Guard Room. Lavish entertainment was, however, infrequent. More often than not, it was a glass of red wine of indifferent vintage and a sausage roll consumed while standing and attempting to keep out of the way of the more aggressive members of the General Synod.

On these domestic occasions the Chaplain would be required to protect his employer from the many requests directed towards him. On the domestic front alone there was a great deal for a new Chaplain to learn. A young man plucked from the leafy byways of Marlborough and transported into the Byzantine labyrinth of Lambeth might well feel that his knowledge of public school politics paled into insignificance when it came to dealing with his new job. The domestic front was complex enough, but of course that was only half the story. There was also the world beyond the Palace walls, indeed beyond the shores of England. The whole Anglican Communion beckoned and demanded that the Archbishop made time to dine at their table, or at the very least to consume their indifferent wine and savoury pastries. Naturally, the Chaplain was expected to stand by his employer on such foreign tours too.

145

Although in my day none of the Chaplains lodged in the Water Tower, Richard Chartres did live in another tower in the Palace, access to which was gained by ascending a very narrow flight of stairs. He was a man of iron discipline who lived a frugal life and, it is reputed, slept on the floor of his cell-like quarters. His worthy successor, John Witheridge, being married at the time of his appointment, was spared the steep climb to the roof and was given a comfortable billet in the old stable block. I hasten to add that the former barn had been converted into living quarters fit for clergy, and might be described as being 'suitable'.

It was a sad day for all when the Chaplain who occupied the tower and allegedly slept on the floor announced that pastures new called and he was leaving the service of his Archbishop. I had made many a convivial journey with him across the globe and had grown to appreciate his ready wit and considerable diplomatic skill. During his long years of service he had explored some of the remoter regions of the Communion and had gained an extensive knowledge of Anglican life and practice. Shortly before he rolled up his bedding and vacated his turret, his chosen successor John arrived on the scene. He appeared to be an amiable chap. His background was in education and he had served a curacy at Luton Parish Church in the centre of the town. Within a matter of days, he and his family moved into the old stable block and began to adjust themselves to a completely new way of life.

Much had changed in Lambeth Palace since the happy days of formal dining and scholarly exegesis. I have not studied the travel diary of the late Dr Cornwallis, but I think it extremely unlikely that he travelled much beyond the shores of the

British Isles. He may have made an excursion across the English Channel, but that would have been about his limit. Archbishop Fisher, by contrast, eschewed this sedentary existence when he set forth to explore the wider world of Anglicanism. Admittedly, he went by ship and thus found ample time to study in between eating a hearty breakfast, sipping hot Bovril, partaking of a light lunch, glancing at afternoon tea, sipping a modest cocktail and consuming a substantial dinner. He may have been further tempted by the delights of deck tennis, but I think that unlikely as he did engage in some substantial writing whilst on the high seas. (His substantial eating, of course, is merely my conjecture.)

Such modest pleasures were denied Dr Runcie and his staff. Each departure for a distant outpost of the Anglican Communion saw us making our way hurriedly to the Alcock and Brown suite at Heathrow, knowing only too well that reheated refreshments and a sleepless night were all that separated us from foreign soil.

I met with the new Chaplain to discuss the Archbishop's forthcoming visit to Uganda. It was a country that I knew well, having lived there as a young man. 'Have you visited Africa?' I asked.

'Well, no,' replied the Chaplain.

His reply did not surprise me. Africa was a bit off the beaten track in those days unless one had been there with Voluntary Service Overseas or had had enough money to splash out on a bucket-and-spade outing to Mombasa.

'Not to worry,' I said cheerfully. 'It's not all that different from many other developing parts of the world. Where have you travelled to?'

'Well,' he said slowly, 'I visited France once, but I'm afraid that it was only a short trip with the school. That's about it, really.'

I did not immediately respond to this. I toyed with the idea of suggesting that he take himself off to the Water Tower and begin work at once on a new Commentary on the Apocrypha. Archbishop Sutton would have been delighted with this man.

'Ah,' I said after a short silence.

Uganda was yet another fast-growing part of the Communion. It was a land of saints, martyrs and CMS missionaries; it was the land where Bishop Tucker met his end; the land where Speke stumbled across the source of the Nile; the land where people were so devout that nothing less than a three-hour sermon would even begin to meet their spiritual needs. Archbishop Runcie was due to preach at least a dozen times in this fertile vineyard and someone had to prepare the outlines for his edifying homilies.

'Ah,' I said again, realizing that I was beginning to sound as if I was visiting the doctor with a severe case of laryngitis. 'You'll need to do a bit of preparation,' I said. 'You know the sort of thing – skim a few books, mug up on the history of the Church Missionary Society, that sort of thing. I'll see what I can dig out for you...'

I returned to my study a worried man. I could manage the briefing files, of which there were many. My long-suffering secretary could take care of the travel arrangements. I could plot the itinerary, attempt to keep in touch with the Archbishop of Uganda (who rarely answered letters, for the simple reason that they hardly ever got through to him) and deal with the Uganda High Commission in London. But to write outlines for all the sermons as well was a bit too much. I would simply have to hope for the best. Books were duly sought and, being the diligent fellow that he was, the new Chaplain worked through them. Advice was requested from the Revd Sam, and he obligingly deluged the Palace with files, folders and manuscripts.

Finally the day of departure dawned. Weighed down with all the paraphernalia required for a major archiepiscopal visit, we made our way to Heathrow. 'If only we were travelling by ship,' I said wistfully, to no one in particular. 'What bliss that would be. Two whole weeks at least to strengthen ourselves before engaging with the missionary warriors.'

The Chaplain clutched his portable typewriter. 'I shall have to work on the plane,' he muttered. 'What with moving into the house, sorting the kids out, finding my way about Lambeth, there hasn't been a moment.' I sympathized with him. Times had certainly changed since old Cornwallis tucked into his steak pudding alongside his trusty Chaplain.

My memory of the journey has faded with the passing of the years. I recollect slipping into a light slumber as my diligent companion tapped away through the long night hours, while the Archbishop attempted to make some sense of briefing file number one. I awoke as dawn was breaking. The Chaplain had succumbed to sleep halfway through an address and was slumped over his portable typewriter. I suspected that the congregation for whom it was intended would be similarly inclined.

Our plane landed in Nairobi, where we had made arrangements with a missionary organization to fly us the few hundred miles into Entebbe. They were the proud owners of a single-propeller plane, the pilot of which spent much of his time flying in and out of the Congo and other equally remote locations. He was waiting for us on the tarmac.

'I don't much like the look of those clouds,' he said. We cast our eyes heavenwards, not for the last time. 'Looks pretty nasty to me,' he continued. 'We'd better get the luggage on board.'

The Chaplain and I set off, with the Archbishop in tow, to find the lounge. We pushed open the door to a room and found it was full of black African clerics. As we entered, they leapt to their feet and beamed at Dr Runcie. 'I think we're in for an impromptu meeting,' I muttered to the Chaplain. 'One of us had better stay.'

The Chaplain left posthaste to assist the pilot, while I guided the Archbishop to a vacant seat in the corner. 'What's going on?' he whispered to me. 'I didn't expect to see anyone here.'

'None of us did,' I answered. 'Word has clearly got round that you're passing through and they've turned out to greet you. Very civil of them.'

As is often the case with civility, it was also time-consuming. As the storm clouds gathered, the Archbishop sat listening to speech after speech, doing his best to maintain interest in the Church politics of East Africa (not the easiest thing after a long flight).

The Chaplain appeared in the doorway and beckoned to me. 'We must go,' he said urgently. 'If we don't get out now, we'll be trapped by the weather.'

I have frequently marvelled at Dr Runcie's talent for appearing to take a passionate interest in the most mundane of matters. He had that unique ability to make every individual with whom he conversed feel that no other issue was more important than the matter they were bringing before him. Unfortunately, it also meant that Dr Runcie was notoriously difficult to prise out of such a gathering. There were occasions when the good man had to be virtually frog-marched out of a room in order to get him to his next meeting in reasonable time. After many farewells, handshakes, warm embraces and a rousing hymn, the Archbishop was finally eased out onto the tarmac.

In our absence the pilot had stacked suitcases in every available corner slot of the small plane. 'We must be quick,' he said. 'We have to get above those dark clouds before they come any nearer. If we don't, there might be trouble.'

The Chaplain took me to one side. 'I hear,' he said, 'that one of these contraptions came down the other day. The pilot had filled up at some remote airfield and discovered too late that some rogues had been mixing water with the aviation fuel. That won't happen here … will it?'

I assured him that we were as safe as houses in Kenya. I did not tell him of the time some years previously when we were approaching Nairobi Airport and narrowly missed a jumbo jet. Had it not been for the sharp eyes of the Archbishop's press officer who was sitting next to the pilot, we might well have been flipped over by the slipstream.

We clambered aboard and followed the instructions of the pilot to strap ourselves in securely. 'Before I start the engine,' he said, 'I'd like to have a word of prayer.' The Archbishop threw me a nervous glance. 'O Lord,' began the pilot, 'if it be thy will, let us rise above the storm clouds and arrive safely at our destination.'

'And what,' whispered the Chaplain, 'if it not be the Lord's will? What then?'

'I'm not so sure that I believe in such unqualified prayer,' said the Archbishop with a smile.

The engine spluttered into life. We glanced across at the lounge and waved good-bye to the reception party. At last we were bound heavenwards. It took the little plane quite a long time to climb to a decent altitude, no doubt due to the fact that our combined weight plus all the ceremonial kit and gifts put quite a strain on the single engine. 'I'm going up higher!' bellowed the pilot. 'We should then be able to fly right over the storm!'

Suffice it to say that his prayers were answered. We topped the storm, cruised over the Kenyan Highlands and headed for Entebbe. I took the opportunity to deliver a last-minute briefing to His Grace. 'They will have a big turnout for you,' I began. 'Be prepared for lots of singing and dancing. If I know Uganda, there will be hundreds of people at the airport to welcome you.' I went through the list of individuals from Church and State who would be in the line-up: the Archbishop and his numerous staff and extended family; the President and his numerous staff and extended family; more staff and yet more extended families.

'Ten minutes!' yelled the pilot. 'I'll fly over the airport once so that you can catch a sight of the welcoming party from the air.'

We peered through the cabin windows at Lake Victoria. 'That's funny,' shouted the pilot. 'The place seems deserted!' By now we were skimming across the runway. In the distance we could see an obviously deserted airport building. A couple of Africans sitting on a crate looked up at us and did not even trouble to wave.

'Are you sure we've come to the right place?' queried the Chaplain.

I glanced at my watch. Despite our reception party in Kenya, we were on time. I opened the briefing file. We had arrived on the right day. I checked the correspondence. In my last communication to Uganda I had confirmed all the arrangements.

'What shall I do?' asked the pilot.

'If this is Entebbe Airport and not some identical airport in the Congo, then land,' I replied with a touch of irritation in my voice. Frankly I was alarmed. This was the start of an official visit and no one was in sight. The long-suffering pilot did another turn over the lake and pointed the plane in the general direction of the runway.

As we descended, my worst fears were confirmed. The two Africans on the crate were the only sign of life in the whole airport. I unbuckled my harness, jumped down onto the runway and strolled across to them. The air was pleasantly warm. A light breeze blew across the water and apart from the rustling of the wind in the trees it was perfectly silent.

'Jambo,' I said to the relaxing pair, immediately exhausting my knowledge of Swahili. They returned the greeting.

'Is there anyone here?' They nodded in the direction of the control tower.

'What about the welcoming party?' They looked puzzled. 'For the Archbishop of Canterbury,' I added, not that I expected it to make any difference whatsoever. They looked even more puzzled.

'Where is the telephone?' I asked, now feeling very nervous indeed. They directed me to the terminal building.

The Archbishop, the Chaplain and the pilot had descended from the plane and were sheltering from the sun under one of the wings. 'Come on over,' I shouted. 'We'll go inside.'

As the pilot began to unpack the cases, the Chaplain and the Archbishop made their way towards me. We went into the terminal building and looked around. A uniformed individual approached us and hesitated at the sight of the Archbishop, clad in his purple cassock in preparation for a ceremonial greeting.

'Hello,' I said cheerfully. 'Have we arrived too early?' The uniformed man looked puzzled.

'Is the Archbishop of Uganda anywhere around?' I asked, as if expecting the Prelate to be sheltering in one of the luggage lockers.

'No,' replied the uniform. 'Who are you?'

I explained who we were and asked if we might have the use of a telephone. Public telephones were not much in evidence in those days. The uniform made a discreet bow in the general direction of Canterbury, and I was directed to a small office. The Chaplain took himself off to persuade the only reception party in evidence to leave their crate for long enough to see to our luggage.

I shall not trouble the reader with a full account of my efforts to telephone Kampala, some 20 or so miles from the airport. Eventually I was connected with an operator who, after half an hour or so, put me through to the Archbishop's residence. I knew from previous experience that it would be no easy matter to track down a specific individual in his household. Given that there was to be a celebration, relatives from the countryside would have taken over the property and would almost certainly be spending hours on the telephone inviting others to join them.

'Hello,' I said hopefully.

'Hello,' replied a voice.

'Can I speak with the Archbishop, please?' I continued optimistically.

'Hello,' said the voice.

'Hello,' I repeated. 'The Archbishop, please.'

'Wait.'

There was a great deal of chattering in the background, mingled with the cries of young children and an occasional animal. Another voice came on the line.

'Hello,' it said.

'Hello,' I replied, somewhat wearily. 'The Archbishop, please.'

'Wait.'

Thanking my lucky stars that I was not in a coinbox, I awaited the next voice. By nothing less than an act of God, it was the Archbishop himself.

'Ah, Terry,' he said. 'Where are you?'

I told him. There was a silence. '*Where*?'

Someone dropped a saucepan in the background and there were loud cries of alarm, intermingled with yet more animal noises. I could hear the Archbishop telling someone off in his local dialect. He returned to the receiver. 'But it's tomorrow you arrive,' he said.

I detected a note of distress in his voice, but this was no time for debate. I explained that we were at the airport and it would be good if we might be collected.

'We'll be there very soon!' he shouted. It sounded as though some kind of fight had broken out around him. He seemed to be attempting to speak with me and mediate all at the same time. 'Just wait there! My son works at the airport. He might be at home. I'll phone him to get round to you quickly!' There was a crash, as though the telephone had been dropped, and the line went dead.

While I had been speaking, my two companions had joined me in the office. Word had clearly got around that the Archbishop of Canterbury had arrived, and a small group of Africans had appeared from nowhere in particular and were gazing at us through the window.

The Archbishop seemed to have accepted the situation with the weary resignation born of long experience. 'Don't worry,' I said, attempting to reassure myself. 'Some mistake with the date. It happens all the time here.'

Someone came in with some tea and we sipped it grate-fully. I was conscious of the fact that this was the Chaplain's first overseas tour, indeed his first real visit abroad. He did not look too impressed, although, being good natured, he was amused. 'Bit of a shambles, eh?' he said. 'What's gone wrong?'

'I haven't a clue,' I muttered. 'Communications are diffi-cult and there has been some almighty mix-up. It'll be fine. It always is, eventually.'

It was. We were ushered away from the group of onlookers into a more comfortable room, and there we waited. Within the hour the door burst open and the rotund, perspiring figure of the Archbishop of Uganda appeared. 'Your Grace!' He beamed at Canterbury. 'I'm so very sorry. I don't know what happened!'

'It's Waite's fault,' said Dr Runcie. 'Never could get these things right. He got me to the wrong airport in America once. I do hope we've not inconvenienced you, Archbishop.'

The two Prelates of the Church embraced like the brothers they were and walked out towards the car. I turned to the Chaplain. 'This,' I said, 'is but the first chapter. There is more to come, I assure you. Much more.'

We trudged behind the truck carrying the luggage into the warmth of the welcoming sun. The two senior Churchmen strolled to their car. An old fellow with a straw hat doffed it in their general direction. Before us lay the dusty red road leading into Kampala. Despite the unfortunate arrival, it was good to be back on African soil.

* * * * *

My expectations were fulfilled when we arrived at the Archbishop's residence, constructed in the days when the Episcopalians in the United States were prepared to spend some money in Africa. Some argued that it was a very handsome edifice, and indeed it would have looked well overlooking the ocean in Florida. As a house for an African Archbishop, however, it left something to be desired. No provision had been made for the country cousins, the dining room was tiny and there were certainly not enough bedrooms. As for the kitchen, the less said the better.

A visit by the Archbishop of Canterbury had attracted relatives and friends from every part of the nation, which explained most of the background noises on the telephone. Relatives were everywhere. They lingered in the hallway, sat on the stairs and totally swamped the cubbyhole which masqueraded as the kitchen. In the back garden young men were busy rolling huge cooking pots into place. Several others wielded axes as they chopped branches for the fire.

'Come on in,' said the Archbishop, as he pushed his way through the throng. 'You will all be staying here.'

A goat poked its nose through an open window and received a smart smack on the head for its trouble. 'Take him away!' shouted the Archbishop to one of the many helpers milling around in the garden.

The Archbishop's wife appeared and beamed at everyone. She was a large, genial lady dressed in the traditional costume of the region, introduced by the Victorian missionaries in the nineteenth century. She did not speak, partly through modesty and partly because her command of English was not extensive. As we stood surveying the scene of frantic activity, several young men struggled up the stairs with our luggage. We followed. Archbishop Runcie was shown into one of the bedrooms and the Chaplain and I were asked if we would share another. That left just one further room for the permanent occupants of the house and several dozen relatives.

The Chaplain walked across to the window. 'Good heavens!' he exclaimed. 'Look out here. It's like Noah's Ark.'

Down below, cattle, goats, sheep and chickens mingled in seemingly contented confusion. 'That's tomorrow's dinner,' I said. 'The Archbishop will have to cater for his relatives and half of Uganda by the looks of it.'

The Chaplain turned slightly pale. 'Do you mean they're going to kill those animals here?'

'Don't worry,' I said. 'They won't begin until after dark and if you don't like meat, there'll be plenty of plantain. It's very good with groundnut sauce.'

'It's not that I don't like meat,' he replied. 'It's the thought of all that going on beneath our bedroom window.' He sat on the bed, took out his portable typewriter and began to tap away.

'Better to get on with things now,' I said. 'It's bound to get noisy later.' He gave me a wry look and continued with his work.

As anticipated, it was a disturbed night. There was a great deal of coming and going down in the garden and when we awoke, several iron cauldrons were steaming away merrily.

'This is not quite what I expected,' said the Chaplain as we sat together at breakfast. 'What's on the programme today?'

Today, of course, was the day we were due to arrive in Kampala – according to the local schedule, that is. 'Later this afternoon,' I replied, 'we're off to see the Roman Catholic Cardinal Archbishop for a courtesy call. Apparently he's very keen to meet Dr Runcie.'

One of the many traditions in Africa was that the head-man in the region lived at the top of the hill – assuming, of course, that there were hills to live on top of. Kampala was well supplied, since, like Rome, it was built on seven of them. The Anglicans took pride of place on one of these and, quite naturally, the Roman Catholics perched on one of the others. Late in the afternoon we prepared ourselves for the first visit of our stay. I rummaged in one of our cases to find the gift we had brought for the Cardinal. The two Archbishops decked themselves out in their best purple cassocks, and the Chaplain donned a white garment especially made for visits to tropical climes.

For the duration of our visit, the Archbishop of Uganda had been able to persuade the government to loan him a couple of Mercedes. At the appointed time we made our way through the assembled relatives and kitchen assistants and out to the front of the house. Quite a sizeable crowd had gathered outside the gates and at the sight of the two Church leaders they let out a tremendous cheer, equal if not superior to the greeting we had experienced in Nigeria. This was merely a foretaste of what was to come.

The cars moved slowly through the gates and set off in the direction of the Roman Catholic hill. The route was lined with flag-waving enthusiasts, delighted, no doubt, to have something to celebrate. We slowly ascended the hill towards the twin-towered cathedral. Here hundreds of schoolchildren had been recruited to join the flag-wavers. The Chaplain expressed surprise. 'I've never seen anything like it,' he said in amazement. 'Do they know who it is they're cheering?'

I told him, somewhat cynically, that it was very unlikely but it did not matter. They clearly enjoyed it, we enjoyed it, and the old Cardinal certainly enjoyed it, as he was no doubt responsible for arranging the massive turnout. It was a wonderful display of strength.

Our driver carefully negotiated the crowds milling around the cathedral steps and brought the car to a halt. A small group of musicians struck up on what seemed to be home-made instruments and produced a home-made noise. This was quickly extinguished by further cheering. The Cardinal, his face shining with perspiration and pleasure, slowly descended the steps and embraced the Archbishops before leading Dr Runcie into the cathedral. After a suitable interval, they returned to the door and once again massive cheering reverberated across the city. The Cardinal positioned himself before a microphone.

'Beware,' I said to the Chaplain. 'I have yet to attend a public function where the public address system didn't cause trouble.'

My record was not to be broken. The Cardinal began to speak and immediately a thousand electronic banshees drowned out his words. In time-honoured fashion, he tapped the microphone and the crowds were able to hear the sound of his amplified index finger perfectly. He resumed speaking and back came the banshees. After a hasty consultation with several home-made technicians and after receiving instructions to hold the microphone at least two feet away from his mouth, the old man was able to speak without interruption. He greeted Dr Runcie with warmth and affection. Given the fact that relations between the Anglicans and Catholics had in the past left much to be desired, this was a moving moment. Dr Runcie responded with equal generosity of spirit.

Now came the moment for the exchange of gifts. The Cardinal beckoned and a young man staggered forward carrying a sizeable package. It was revealed to be a painting which, when shown to the crowd, was received with considerable acclaim. It portrayed an enigmatic Dr Runcie staring, Mona Lisa fashion, into the middle distance. Dr Runcie made pleasurable noises and handed over some trinkets from Canterbury.

As we retreated into an inner sanctum for some light refreshment, the Archbishop of Canterbury expressed a desire to meet and thank the painter of his impressive new acquisition. A young man was summoned into the presence of the Churchmen.

'It's marvellous,' said the Archbishop with enthusiasm. 'How did you manage to paint such a portrait in such a short time? The Cardinal tells me that you only had a few days to complete it.'

The young man beamed. 'It was easy,' he said proudly. 'Last year when the Pope visited I painted two pictures of him. As I had one over, I painted out the Pope's face and painted yours in.'

Dr Runcie looked taken aback at this unexpected revelation, but he nodded his approval with commendable aplomb.

The Chaplain and I collected this remarkable example of African ecumenism and made arrangements for it to be transported back to Lambeth. Farewells were said to the Cardinal and his enterprising artist and we returned through the cheering crowd to our car.

'Not quite Luton, is it?' I said as the Chaplain resumed his typing.

'It's interesting,' he said. 'Very interesting.'

13

A Papal Address

The late Edward Carpenter, one-time Dean of Westminster, once wrote a book charting the lives of the Archbishops of Canterbury. Dr Carpenter was a learned and kindly man. I have memories of him cycling through the streets of London with his trousers tucked into his woollen socks, like a fugitive from Cambridge. He began, naturally enough, with Augustine and concluded with a mention of Dr Michael Ramsey, the one-hundredth Archbishop of Canterbury. Dr Runcie was the one-hundred-and-second holder of the office and this illuminating detail was often communicated by his staff throughout the Anglican Communion whenever it was necessary to impress the locals.

Dr Carpenter reminded his readers that in the Middle Ages the Archbishop of Canterbury was clearly the Pope's man. If we exclude Reginald Pole, William Warham was the last Archbishop who died with the Pope as his boss. Archbishop William was a sad man, as his portrait indicates. He had every reason to be. He was up against the scheming Wolsey, and he had to cope with Henry VIII. He also had many a run-in with his clergy. I make mention of all this because, following Warham, relations between Canterbury and Rome cooled considerably. Four hundred years later, Archbishop Ramsey warmed them up a little. His successor Donald Coggan let them simmer, and Dr Runcie turned up the heat a little further.

Dr Runcie was by no means a Papist, though he inclined towards what is fondly known within the Anglican Communion as 'High Church', had no objection to a few bells and incense and was quite happy to wear colourful clothing in church. He got on perfectly well with the Cardinal Archbishop of Westminster, but then again, as we saw earlier, he was also completely happy to share a dram with the Moderator of the Church of Scotland. In other words, Dr Runcie was an old-fashioned liberal, and his liberal tendencies led him to seek an early meeting with the successor of those who had so frequently meddled with English affairs, namely the Bishop of Rome.

This did get him into trouble from time to time, as indicated by his famous encounter with the Revd Jack Glass. Dr Ian Paisley was also none too impressed. On one memorable occasion, when hard words were being traded between the two Divines, Dr Runcie invited the fearsome Ulsterman to meet him in the Palace. Inadvertently he suggested that Dr Paisley might care to 'walk across the water' to visit him. All Dr Runcie was proposing was that Dr Paisley might cross from Westminster to Lambeth via the bridge, but certain mischievous souls insinuated that the Archbishop was in fact challenging the good Doctor to emulate a well-known miracle.

Dr Runcie was prepared to meet with all and sundry and His Holiness the Pope was high on the list. In common with all meetings between those who hold high office, secular or divine, there were diplomatic considerations to be taken into account. Archbishop Ramsey had visited Rome to seek an improvement in the relationship between the two Churches. His successor had done the same. After 400 years of frost, however, it was not surprising that they only succeeded in bringing about a minor thaw. It was a thaw nonetheless, and was welcomed by some and regretted by others. There were many who considered it inappropriate for yet another new Archbishop of Canterbury to be seen heading for Fumicino Airport as soon as his feet were under the Lambeth table. It smacked a bit too much of the days when oaths were sworn and the Holy Father bestowed the sheepskin pallium on the incoming Archbishop.

It has been said on more than one occasion that the Roman Catholic Church has the best placed intelligence agents in the world, and the worst retrieval system. There was one particular occasion, however, when the retrieval system proved more than adequate.

One day an agent in the field reported a rumour that His Holiness the Pope was planning a visit to West Africa. This was valuable information, as Dr Runcie was also considering a visit to the great continent at that time. The fact that the proposed visit by the Archbishop was to Zaire, not West Africa, was not important. It would be easy for Dr Runcie to meet with the Pope in the west of the continent and then slip away into the bush to celebrate with Anglicans from one of the more modest areas of Church growth in Africa.

Dr Runcie was not slow to recognize the value of meeting the Pope on African soil. Low Church Anglicans would not be able to say that yet another Archbishop was off to Rome to pay homage. The two leaders would be able to meet as brothers in a fast-growing part of the ecclesiastical world and put their heads (and perhaps their hands) together on, as some like to call it, a level playing field.

The Archbishop, always conscious of diplomatic relations, communicated first with Cardinal Hume, his Roman Catholic counterpart in England. The Cardinal had recently been appointed to his position of eminence within the Roman Catholic Church and was barely acquainted with the Holy Father. Courteous at all times, he expressed pleasure that his brother Archbishop was being given an opportunity for a personal conversation with His Holiness before he had been given an extended audience himself.

Preparations were put in train. Reports from our men in Rome indicated that the Holy Father would be visiting Ghana. As far as I was concerned this was a happy coincidence, as the country was well known to me and that fact might ease somewhat the preparations necessary for our visit.

So far, only two members of the Archbishop's private staff have figured prominently in these tales – the Chaplain and myself. There were many others, of course. A layman, wise in the workings of government, guided the Archbishop through the complexities of the House of Lords. A press officer laboured diligently to project and protect His Grace on every flank. Across the Lambeth courtyard two or three scholarly individuals pored over documents emanating from their involvement in ecumenical affairs and advised their employer accordingly. Also, of course, there was the Bishop at Lambeth, who had relinquished his position of authority in a diocese in favour of attempting the impossible, namely to co-ordinate the work of the several specialist advisors to the Archbishop. Only one of these need concern us at the moment and that is the Archbishop's Advisor on Ecumenical Matters. A visit with the Pope clearly demanded specialist attention, and one of the bright clerics from across the courtyard was summoned by the Archbishop and invited to come up with some smart ideas and workable proposals.

Back in the Palace itself, the Chaplain and I put our heads together. Clearly we were going to have to engage the services of the missionary air force once again. Getting to Ghana was simple enough, but travelling from Ghana to the far side of Zaire was another matter altogether and the missionary pilots would certainly be required for that leg of the journey.

Finally, all was arranged and the day of departure dawned. Thanks to the diligent work of the ecumenical scholar, the final details of the meeting were confirmed and we were all set to go. It had also been arranged for the Archbishop and his party to stay with the British High Commissioner in Accra. This time, a slightly larger party was assembled for the journey. It consisted of the Chaplain, a couple of Lambeth ecumenical experts, the press officer and myself. The extra members departed early to prepare the ground in Ghana. The Archbishop, his Chaplain and I travelled together with John Brown to Heathrow.

London's principal airport is an ever-developing organism and ought to be an example to rapidly expanding Anglicans everywhere. The place was occupied by workmen in hard hats at least 50 years ago, and they and their descendants have been diligently expanding the place ever since. We drove through numerous building sites, along a perimeter fence and finally arrived at a VIP suite hidden behind several Portakabins. We stumbled from the car, smiled at the photographers and entered the building. The majority of those who staffed the VIP suite had been working there for many years and were in fact diplomats of the highest order. Should they ever have had the misfortune to be made redundant, they could easily have been able to find a job at the UN, dealing with the swarms of status-conscious individuals who throng that building.

The VIP suite was rather like a superior club lounge, except that there was no bar in evidence. The staff of the suite carefully placed their charges in convenient corners of the room and then brought to them whatever was required. Dr Runcie, being a man of modest habits, normally ordered a refreshing cup of tea and of course his staff, though longing for a gin and tonic, followed his good example.

I cast my eyes around the room. In one corner lurked several Middle Eastern VIPs, surrounded by large men wearing padded suits. In another corner three superior-looking Europeans, clearly UN types, sipped their cocktails with looks of mournful resignation in their bloodshot eyes. I guessed they had just arrived overnight from New York and were probably on their way to yet another administrative hell-hole for another round of drinks and fractious conversation.

The staff of the suite had done their work with habitual skill and everyone was given just the right amount of space, according to their status. If deadly enemies were to arrive or depart from Heathrow at the same time, then one group could always be hidden away in a side room or, in cases of emergency, put into another building altogether. I ought to record that the VIP staff were fond of Dr Runcie. They always gave him a great deal of space in the suite and enjoyed many a merry quip with him as he sipped his tea and prepared to board the plane.

The time for embarkation arrived. The VIP minder handed me our passports and we trooped outside to the car for the gentle ride to the plane. Normally we boarded after everyone else was seated, as this caused minimum inconvenience to the airline staff and meant that we could be seated quickly and without trouble. The journey passed pleasantly enough and within a few hours we were walking across a rather steamier stretch of tarmac to the airport building in Accra.

Ghanaians are, in my experience, cheerful people. I first knew the country when it was suffering severe economic hardship and have memories of entering a supermarket in the capital and being shocked to find that there were only a few bottles of sauce and some scrubbing brushes on sale. One might have imagined that the manager of the store would have been cast deep in gloom at the desultory state of his establishment. Far from it. As I entered he beamed as though he was in charge of Fortnum & Mason. There was only a handful of customers in the store and, despite the fact that the cash registers were silent, they were beaming also.

Cars were waiting at the airport to drive us to the residence of the British High Commissioner. I think it proper at this juncture to say a positive word on behalf of these loyal servants of the Commonwealth. There is a notion that our representatives in foreign parts live, to put it simply, the life of Riley. Mention an Ambassador or High Commissioner to the man in the street, and immediately he thinks of gin, expensive chocolates, splendid dinner parties and long, paid holidays. I have to confess that I have enjoyed many a decent gin and tonic in some of our far-flung outposts and have eaten acceptable dinners in more government residences than I care to remember. Whenever it was arranged for Dr Runcie and his party to stay with a British diplomat on our overseas tours I was normally overjoyed, as it meant that we would certainly be given the most considerate care and attention.

Of course, whilst this was fine for us visitors, it was something of a strain for the diplomat and his family. To be hotel manager and host to an endless succession of guests, almost all of whom are not of your own choosing and some of whom are not only surly but downright disagreeable, would tax the patience of the most saintly. The Archbishop, being totally conversant with the fatiguing aspects of enforced geniality, was aware of this fact and, along with his staff, remained grateful for such sanctuary in the midst of a demanding programme.

Our host on this occasion did not disappoint. He hailed from Scotland and, appropriately enough for our visit, subscribed to the Catholic faith as interpreted by the Romans. Thus he was more than pleased that his particular neck of the woods, which would not be considered the most significant of diplomatic postings, was to be the setting for the first meeting between the Archbishop of Canterbury and his own spiritual supremo.

I have made mention of the fact that the Roman Catholic Church has its agents in virtually every corner of the globe. It ought also to be revealed that the Holy Father has his own personal special agents there too, in the form of the Papal Nuncio. There was a time when all holders of this high office were Italians and I imagine that today there continue to be a fair proportion of Latins in the ranks. Relations between the Pope's man and the local Bishops vary. At times they can be most cordial, but in countries where perhaps the local holder of the episcopal office is still finding his feet following the departure of European missionaries, there can be tensions. To know that the Nuncio is watching every move and might be reporting in considerable detail to the Secretary of State in the Vatican is enough to cause the most confident of Bishops to think twice before kicking over the traces.

On his visit to Ghana the Pope, in his wisdom, was to reside at the home of his agent the Nuncio, and it was agreed that the meeting between Canterbury and Rome should take place in that very establishment. Fortunately for all concerned, the Nuncio appeared to be an amiable chap who got on well with the locals, so we were all spared any tedious infighting.

The home of the Nuncio in Accra turned out to be a modest establishment. It was newly built and I believe that the Nuncio was in fact the first occupant. A secure fence surrounded the compound and large iron gates protected the entrance. These elementary precautions were necessary in Ghana, as the country had its fair share of thieves and brigands who would not think twice about relieving the most humble cleric of his worldly possessions, let alone the Papal Nuncio. The inside of the house was furnished in the style beloved by Italian Prelates: some marble (though not too much), some rather good furniture, several religious pictures and a few decent carpets. It was tasteful without being ostentatious.

The morning of the meeting arrived. We had enjoyed a restful night following an evening of generous hospitality from the High Commissioner. I recollect that the Archbishop retired early, leaving the Chaplain and myself to enjoy a little late-night refreshment with His Excellency before we retired ourselves. The morning was, as is frequently the case in Africa, bright and sunny. Our first visitor, who appeared shortly after breakfast, was none other than our man in Accra, the local Anglican Bishop. In keeping with the Ghanaian character, he was cheerful, and as befitted his status, he was also somewhat rotund. He had put on his best finery for the occasion. The gigantic white cassock would certainly have provided shelter for many of his flock in the event of a natural disaster. A broad purple sash was fastened around his generous waist, and a purple skullcap was perched on his cheerful head.

He rolled into the room and greeted the Archbishop in the time-honoured way, by enfolding him in a warm embrace. As this was Dr Runcie's first visit to Ghana, he had not previously met the Bishop and so the two fathers of the Church retired to a quiet corner so that the Bishop might communicate some local intelligence to His Grace. Meanwhile, the Chaplain and I discussed the timetable for the forthcoming meeting. The arrangements had been left to the ecumenical expert from Lambeth and his opposites from Rome. It had been decided that the Pope would first greet everyone and then disappear with the Archbishop for a totally private conversation. There would be no statement of substance issued. All that would be said was that the two leaders had met and – provided they did not come to blows – had enjoyed a cordial conversation.

The time came for the party to leave for the Nuncio's residence and we trooped out to the cars for the dusty drive. There were no flag-waving Anglicans this time, nor flag-waving Catholics for that matter. This was not a visit to stir up the local population. It was simply a diplomatic meeting on African soil. Our cars drove through the iron gates of the humble dwelling and we stepped out. The Nuncio, as genial as his Ghanaian brothers, was on hand to greet us. Following the obligatory embrace, we trooped after him into his modest living room.

He held out his hands in an apologetic gesture. 'It is not so very large,' he said as he surveyed the room. 'But it is in keeping with our situation. The Holy Father is upstairs, but he will be down shortly. You will take some coffee?'

We took some coffee and wandered out onto the small terrace to drink it. The Nuncio was in the early stages of taming his garden. It was a fairly small plot and bore all the signs of having been tidied up in great haste after the departure of the builders, who, in my experience, have little respect for or knowledge of matters horticultural. As there was a notable absence of trees, and as the African sun was climbing rapidly in the sky, we retreated fairly soon to the relative cool of the living room. By now quite a little party had gathered. The Nuncio had been reinforced by one or two ecclesiastics, who were busy exchanging notes with our ecumenical expert.

One of the papal company stepped forward. 'The Holy Father will be down in a moment. He will first of all greet you, Your Grace.' He nodded respectfully towards the Archbishop. 'Then, if Your Grace would be so kind as to introduce members of your delegation to the Holy Father, he would be very pleased. After that, perhaps you might leave for a totally private conversation with His Holiness.'

It all seemed very civilized and no objections were raised. I half suspected that the Holy Father had been hiding behind the door, for no sooner had this little speech been delivered than it opened and in came the great man himself. He was dressed in a rather superior white cassock which made the garment worn by Dr Runcie look unhappily like a cheap imitation. No matter: the Pope normally wore white, while the Archbishop only pulled his out of the wardrobe when a visit to warmer climes beckoned. Clearly, the Pope needed a quality garment for everyday use.

I should mention that this historic encounter took place before a gunman almost took the life of the Pontiff. He looked fit and hearty and there was a merry twinkle in his eyes. He immediately walked towards the Archbishop and made what I took to be Polish noises of pleasure. 'Ahhh, Archbishop Runcie...'

His distinctive tones reverberated around the room, causing much Italian, Ghanaian and English cheer. The Archbishop greeted him warmly and led him along the small line-up. The

Pope stopped for a brief word with each individual and, before moving on, stretched out his hand to collect a small gift from his secretary which he handed over. Each person received a small medallion and a rosary.

The Archbishop led him towards me. 'This is my assistant, Terry Waite. He has a great deal of African experience.' I'm not sure just how much the Holy Father had mastered the English language at this stage in his Pontificate. However, he nodded wisely, exchanged a few words and continued to hand over the trophies.

Then the two wise men left the living room and ascended the stairs to a secluded room the Nuncio had provided for their conversation. Meanwhile, we took more coffee and chatted amongst ourselves.

After some considerable time, we heard footsteps and back they came for a repeat performance. This time it was Dr Runcie's turn to hand over a small gift. Then the Pope shook hands with everyone once again. He came back to me. 'Goodbye, African Experience,' he said with a merry chuckle. 'Goodbye.'

Back in the car, the Archbishop told us that the Pope was not too well acquainted with the most widely distributed group of Christians in the world – the Anglicans – but he had accepted an invitation to visit Canterbury. The visit had achieved what we had set out to achieve, namely to give the two men an opportunity to get to know each other.

When we returned to London, the Archbishop immediately got on the phone to Cardinal Hume. 'I'm delighted to hear that the meeting went so well,' said the Cardinal. 'Quite delighted. What I can't understand is why you met in a car.'

175

Archbishop Runcie, himself a little hard of hearing, was quick to understand and respond. 'Accra!' he shouted. 'Accra, not a car!'

The Pope did come to Canterbury and became much more knowledgeable about the Anglican Communion. He even got to travel with the Archbishop in a very superior motor car, but that is a story for another time.

14

A Couple of Koalas

There was a time when the non-Aboriginal residents of Australia were heartily sick of being reminded of their errant forefathers. How times have changed. Today it is regarded as a mark of distinction to have at least one ancestor who fell foul of the authorities in the UK, and any self-respecting Aussie will claim several. Not all the early settlers were convicts, of course. Some emigrated of their own accord to carve out a bright new future for themselves – and if they were slightly disappointed in what they found, they were careful what they told the folks back home.

'Now father,' wrote a young Yorkshire lad in 1848, 'I think this is the Promised Land, but there are faults in it.' His proud parent promptly sent the letter to the *Bradford Observer* and they printed it in the December of that year.

Charles Darwin was not so diplomatic. As he hauled up the sail on HMS *Beagle*, he muttered, 'Farewell, Australia! You are a rising child, and doubtless some day will reign a great princess in the South; but you are too great and ambitious for affection, yet not great enough for respect. I leave your shores without sorrow or regret.' One can only assume that there was a fair wind blowing at the time to hasten his departure, otherwise he might have left the country with a bloody nose and an enhanced understanding of the species residing in that great southern land.

The Archbishop had received numerous requests to pay a full-scale visit to Australia. As far as I know, he had no Australian relatives, nor do I believe that any of his ancestors were convicts. The Anglican Church was well established in the country, however, and a full-scale visit was undoubtedly required. Earlier he had done the honours for New Zealand and had stopped for a couple of days in Sydney on his way back to London. That was hardly a grand tour, and Lambeth received frequent demands from Perth, Melbourne and other distant places for the Primate of All England to 'come on down'. We all knew it was going to be exhausting. Clearly it would be impossible to cover every part of the country, but we needed to visit the main centres of population as well as one or two bush locations. Preparations were put in train, and in no time at all John Brown was loading the car for Heathrow Airport.

At this juncture a little ecclesiastical background might be helpful. Within the Church an Archbishop has responsibility for a province. Within a province there are numerous dioceses, each with a Bishop running the shop. A diocese consists of a collection of parishes. (There are intermediate units of admin- istration, but it is unnecessary to give such details here.) Some countries, Australia being one, have several provinces and thus boast several Archbishops. In England there are two provinces, York and Canterbury.

The question of whether the two Archbishops are equal or whether one is superior to the other has been a matter of long-standing debate. An amusing episode took place, for example, at a Church Council held in Westminster in the twelfth century. The two Archbishops were in dispute regard- ing precedence and the Papal Legate was sent over from Rome to mediate. The then Archbishop of Canterbury took his seat in Council at the right hand of the Legate, a move that sug- gested precedence. Archbishop Roger of York then arrived and attempted 'to squeeze his buttocks' between the Archbishop and the Legate, thus landing on the Primate's lap. It is said that Canterbury's aides intervened and threw the Archbishop of York to the ground. Apparently, when the King heard about this incident, he laughed, as any sensible monarch might. The whole question regarding precedence was discussed by the French scholar Archille Luchaire, who said that there were 'objective' Primates who were able to exercise authority over other Archbishops and 'subjective' ones whose authority was confined to their own province.

Our visit to Australia took us first of all to Brisbane for, to use the ancient terminology, that is where the 'objective' Primate in Australia resided. The 'subjective' brothers were in

179

Perth, Melbourne and Sydney. I doubt whether any of them cared a fig for the historical wranglings described above, but it helps to explain why we visited 'senior' Archbishop John in Brisbane first of all.

It was a bright, sunny day when we arrived. The demolition men, presumably having completed their work in Wellington, had now occupied Brisbane and were busy razing to the ground many of the buildings so carefully erected by industrious Victorian immigrants. The Archbishop lived near the centre of town in a pleasant house that had somehow escaped the attention of the levellers. The Archbishop of Brisbane was not physically large. He hovered somewhere nearer five feet than six, was clean shaven, and the top of his head was exposed to the fierce Australian sun, his hair having disappeared some time ago. We had received a severe warning about the sun in Australia and, along with the rest of the population, had taken the sensible precaution of wearing floppy straw hats to protect us from untold horrors in later life.

Archbishop John possessed a pastoral staff, of course, but he did not walk through the streets of Brisbane with it since most Australian sheep were to be found in the country areas. He only carried it when his flock gathered in the cathedral, or when he attended a church for a formal visit. He had emigrated to Australia from England many years previously and before being ordained had been employed as an accountant. He entered the Anglican Church and, like many an accountant in secular life, quickly rose to the top. It was an impressive and encouraging story. As far as I know, the reasons for his departure from the British Isles were perfectly honourable, and he maintained regular contact with his 90-year-old mother who still lived back in the old country.

'There is one thing I would like to get over with rather quickly,' he said when we were enjoying a cup of tea at his residence. 'The local newspaper is rather anxious to get an exclusive photograph of you, Robert, settling into Australia. Something that can be sent across the country.'

This seemed a very reasonable request. There had been the usual photographers at the airport, but a picture of His Grace of Canterbury out and about in the Commonwealth would no doubt cheer the hearts of many (British MPs except-ed, of course – *they* thought he should stay at home more).

'I think it might be a good thing if we could have a photograph that would instantly make it clear that you are in Australia. A picture that could be printed in a newspaper in any part of the world and communicate that fact.'

We listened to the Archbishop intently. What exactly had he in mind? I had visions of him producing a broad-brimmed hat festooned with corks for Dr Runcie to wear.

The Metropolitan outlined his idea for us. 'I've been in touch with the local zoo,' he said, 'and provided you have no objection, they will arrive shortly with a couple of koalas.'

Dr Runcie raised his eyebrows slightly, but only slightly. Long experience of publicity photography had accustomed him to unusual situations and, to his credit, he normally fell in line and submitted to such requests, as long as they were not totally outlandish.

'Koalas look passive,' continued the Archbishop, 'but in

fact they can be temperamental. They have very sharp claws as they climb trees rapidly, and they can bite.'

This sounded rather alarming. The last thing any of us wanted was for the Archbishop of Canterbury to suffer a mauling at the paws of that gentle and amiable symbol of the great Australian nation. That would not improve relations one jot. When Archbishop John resumed speaking, however, it was clear that he was simply giving the Primate the bad news first.

'However,' he said, 'I think that these two chaps from the zoo will have been given a very slight sedative. Nothing harmful, just a touch of something to make sure that they don't scamper all over the place once they're in the garden.'

His Grace of Canterbury was nodding his head. Being the courteous man that he was, he was always loath to go against the wishes of his host. 'That sounds all right, John,' he said. 'If they prove to be too lively, Waite can manage them, I'm sure.'

I was touched by the faith my employer showed in my ability to calm wild beasts. I promised to do my best, the zoo was telephoned and we were assured that two koalas would be dispatched forthwith. It was early afternoon when a small van rolled up the drive towards the Archbishop's residence. It pulled up under the shade of a large tree and the driver and a photographer climbed out.

'G'day,' said the driver cheerfully. 'The koalas are in the back. They seem fine.'

The photographer began to unload and assemble the numerous tools of his trade. 'I think we should take the pictures under the tree,' he said. 'That will give a bit of shade.'

Meanwhile, the driver of the van had opened the back and was coaxing two somewhat sleepy koalas into the light of day. Had the zoo been a little overenthusiastic with the sedative? 'They'll be fine,' said their keeper, as though he had been reading my thoughts. 'Just sit them on your hip as you would a child. That's all there is to it.'

At that moment a somewhat apprehensive Archbishop appeared from within the house, along with his host. In all the years I had travelled with him I had never observed in him any particular devotion to animals – with the single exception of his pigs, of course. He did not keep a dog or a cat back at home, or even a canary for that matter. I had never for one moment heard him express a dislike of animals, but they did not figure high on his agenda, shall we say. Anyway, he greeted the visitors and made some sort of noise of welcome to the koalas, who blinked at him in return.

'Cheery little fellows, aren't they?' said the keeper. 'Just hold onto them firmly and they'll be fine.'

He placed a koala on my hip. Immediately it grabbed me with its rough paws and held on tightly. The other animal was placed in the Archbishop's charge and that too gripped him as it might the trunk of a tree.

The photographer did what all photographers do the world over, and took far too many pictures. Thankfully the koalas remained passive. The Archbishop appeared satisfied. The next morning the koalas and Dr Runcie took pride of place on the front page of the local newspaper and in no time at all the photograph had circulated the globe. It was a diverting and unusual welcome to Australia, but it had the common touch and that, if one thinks about it, is what Australia is all about.

Our time in Brisbane passed peacefully enough. There was a minor incident when a senior political official made some disparaging remarks about Dr Runcie which were widely reported. I quite forget the content of his utterances, but the individual in question was well known for his extreme opinions and some years later fell from grace. Indeed, if I am not mistaken, he followed the route his forefathers had taken many years previously. Dr Runcie, as becomes a visitor, declined to return the invective and the incident was quickly forgotten.

I think it proper to record here that Archbishop John was a thoughtful and considerate host. He was aware of the pressures and demands made upon those who hold high office and regarded recreational time as being absolutely necessary, even during the course of a national tour. Accordingly he informed us that he had been in touch with several of his nautical friends and, should the Archbishop so desire it, they were willing to take Dr Runcie and his companions out for a day's sea-fishing. Although he came from the seaport of Liverpool and was the offspring of a mother who had spent many years on the high seas (albeit as a hairdresser), Dr Runcie never expressed any great love of the ocean, nor indeed of fishing. Always anxious to please his host, however, he readily agreed and the plans were put into motion.

We were instructed to rise before dawn, since we would need to be well away from port before the sun rose if we were going to have any decent fishing. Archbishop John, for some reason, was not going to join us. The Archbishop, the Chaplain and myself would be entrusted to the competent hands of two or three Aussie fisherfolk, and we would be kept under constant surveillance by a posse of policemen who would keep us in their sights from a boat sailing at a respectful distance from our own craft.

The rest day duly came and in the early morning the three of us set out for the dock. We stepped from the car onto the quay and looked across at our boat for the day. Two or three men wearing shorts and T-shirts and bearing in their girths all the evidence of considerable beer consumption were busy loading crates of the stuff onto the deck. We stepped aboard and took a look around. The boat was quite a reasonable size. There was plenty of fishing tackle and lots of odds and ends that meant nothing to any of us. Down below there was a cosy eating area and a tidy galley within which a cook was already at work on breakfast. As he cooked, he took occasional swigs from a can of beer placed within easy reach.

Now there are breakfasts and Australian breakfasts. Australian breakfasts are truly magnificent. If you can imagine everything you have ever had for breakfast, including steak, all on one plate then you will have an idea of what I am talking about. The cook was busy preparing bacon, sausages, potatoes, mushrooms, eggs, black pudding, steak and kidneys. Already the table was piled high with toast and huge dishes full of butter and marmalade. A large pot of coffee was simmering on the side. As we sat down, the heroic cook opened a cupboard and in a final flourish added a bottle of whisky to this gargantuan repast.

Now, before the good Dr Runcie is pilloried as a glutton and a whisky-bibber, I must report that he ate modestly and drank nothing but coffee. The Chaplain and I, being men of lesser discipline but greater appetite, enjoyed ourselves enormously. As we were eating and conversing with our jolly fisher friends, the deck crew slipped our moorings and by the time we staggered back on deck we were well out to sea and nearing a favourite fishing spot.

Our thoughtful dining companions had carefully prepared several lines and we were handed one each. We were given simple instructions and then told that it was in order to throw them overboard. Almost immediately the Chaplain had a bite and hauled in a decent-sized fish. It was identified immediately, and rather grandly, as a red-finned tricky snapper. The Archbishop and I waited patiently. To our great amazement, no sooner had the Chaplain replaced his bait than he brought in yet another fine specimen. We edged closer to him, hoping to benefit from his good fortune. Alas, this ruse failed to work and he snatched yet another contribution to our lunch while our lines remained motionless.

By now I could see that the Archbishop was getting slightly bored. Remembering the Scriptures, no doubt, he brought in his line and cast off from the other side of the boat. This strategy, which had proved to be so effective for the disciples, brought the successor to the apostles no luck at all. No sooner had he left us than both the Chaplain and I hauled in fish after fish. It was all very rewarding for us and somewhat irritating for our employer. He returned to our side of the boat and handed his line to the Chaplain. 'I think I'll go below and have a short rest,' he said.

We quietly sympathized with him. There was not a lot of fun to be had, standing in the hot sun for hour after hour without so much as a bite. 'I don't think he knows how to fish,' muttered the Chaplain, who was fishing for the first time in his life. 'I'll use his line and see what happens.'

He cast off and before I could even bait my hook there was a tremendous tug on his line. Our ample fisher friends, beer cans at the ready, scurried across the deck and stood by the Chaplain's side. One picked up a landing net while the other issued instructions as to how to play the catch. After at least 20 minutes of intense excitement the net was lowered over the side and a truly enormous fish was landed.

The Chaplain was heartily congratulated for his skill and further cans of beer were given the appropriate treatment by the good-natured Aussie Anglican fishermen. By now the Archbishop had returned on deck to view the Chaplain's prize. He declined an offer to take up his line once more and so we all retired below for a hearty fish lunch, during which the Chaplain was toasted and congratulated once again with considerable enthusiasm. Had our companions been members of the Roman Catholic Church, and had the See of Peter been vacant, he would have been immediately nominated and elevated by common acclaim.

During the long afternoon many of our company took time to recuperate and thus closed their eyes for a space. The police launch pulled alongside and took on board some liquid supplies. Eventually the Captain turned the boat around and headed for home.

When we docked, we found several members of the press corps waiting for us, having been inspired by the amiable photograph of the Archbishop and the koalas. 'Tell us,

Archbishop,' said one of their number, 'how did you enjoy the fishing? Did you land a big one?'

The Archbishop was never one to tell a falsehood willingly. 'I'm pleased to report,' he said confidently, 'that the largest catch of the day was caught on my line.'

The Chaplain, having no desire to leave the Anglican Church or his Chaplaincy, remained silent. It had been a splendid outing for him, for me and for our jovial crew. To this day we remember it with considerable satisfaction.

Having returned to the safety of dry land, and having paid his respects to Archbishop John, the Archbishop packed his case and prepared to leave for the next venue on his tour. This was a remote diocese on the coast of Queensland, still in the province of Archbishop John but under the local oversight of a Bishop.

Queensland can be hot. It can be very hot. It can also be extremely humid. When we pulled into town it was both. Sweat poured off us as we made our way to the diocesan Bishop's house, where we were to stay for a day or so. The Bishop was a lifelong bachelor and rapidly approaching retirement age. He was cared for by a devoted widow who had accommodation on the premises which she shared with her grown-up daughter Barbie. It was altogether a cosy and convenient little arrangement.

The Bishop was a model of courtesy. It was very many years since a personage as eminent as the Archbishop of Canterbury had set foot in his modest wooden bungalow and he was determined to make the visit a success. The widow showed us to our rooms. As befitted the simplicity of the

Bishop's lifestyle, there was no air conditioning in the house, but there was an overhead fan the size of an aeroplane propeller in each bedroom. This proved to be a mixed blessing. It did bring some circulation of air, but it also brought it with such force that unless we kept the briefing papers under strict supervision they were immediately scattered far and wide.

'Phew!' said the Chaplain, who was visiting Australia for the first time. As I may have mentioned, with the notable exception of a day out in France, he was visiting everywhere for the first time. 'I've never experienced heat like this before.'

I must admit that this was one of his least enlightening comments, but it was without doubt accurate. He turned on the fan and rapidly discovered the folly of his ways as papers flew around the room like confetti at a wedding. 'It's all very well staying with the locals,' he muttered as he retrieved his notes, 'but I'm beginning to see why you prefer hotels and High Commissions.'

We had a fitful night. The heat was intense and the fatigue of constant travel was beginning to tell. I rose early and went out into the large sitting area, where Barbie and her devoted mother were busy preparing for breakfast. The mother was dressed, but her daughter was still in her dressing gown. 'Oh,' she cried as I entered, 'for one moment I thought it might be the Archbishop!' She hastily departed and I retreated into the dining room.

The Bishop had already arrived and was examining the table. He was clearly a man who gave himself to detail. The Chaplain and the Archbishop joined us shortly afterwards. I had already noted that the Bishop liked to get things right, but I confess to a little surprise when towards the end of breakfast he produced a small notebook and a pencil. 'Well now, Your Grace,' he said. 'What would you like to drink?'

The Archbishop, having drunk several cups of coffee lovingly prepared by the widow and her daughter, said that he had had sufficient, thank you. The Bishop looked puzzled. 'No,' he said holding up the notebook, 'you misunderstand me. What would you like to drink before dinner this evening?'

There was a long pause as we turned our thoughts from cornflakes and papaya to the cocktail hour. The Archbishop was unaccustomed to ordering alcoholic beverages so early in the morning. In fact, had he made a habit of it, he would have raised many an eyebrow both in Lambeth Palace and through-out the Anglican Communion. The Bishop waited, pencil poised. Finally Dr Runcie was able to focus his thoughts and ordered some simple beverage that would be easily procured.

The Bishop, being a kindly soul, invited a second cousin of my wife to join the company that evening. She had emigrat-ed to Australia many years previously and had distinguished herself by swimming, in record time, a considerable distance between two islands off the coast in a cage, because of sharks. She had not been able to pre-order her drinks, but that did not seem in any way to mar her enjoyment of the evening.

The following day the Archbishop fulfilled various low-key engagements and that was that for Queensland. We said our fond farewells to the household and prepared to con-tinue on our way through that great country so disgracefully maligned by Darwin.

'You know,' said the Chaplain as he packed his case, 'it's good to be on a tour where everything seems to go well.'

I agreed with him. To be a fisher of men was one thing, but to be a fisher of fish was something else altogether. For the Chaplain, Australia was indeed the Promised Land.

15

Home and Away

It is generally expected that an Archbishop of Canterbury, himself the recipient of generous hospitality when travelling abroad, will also be ready to dispense hospitality when at home. Apart from the standard bun fights which were held in Lambeth Palace from time to time, Dr Runcie also did his best to provide a decent sit-down meal for those who visited him from overseas.

These modest repasts were but a pale reflection of the banquets once held in the Palace, of course. The Great Hall at Lambeth was famous for the Consecration Banquets which were held whenever a new Bishop was consecrated in the southern province. In 1367 William of Wykeham put on a feast which, it is reported, 'eclipsed all others in magnificence'. In those days the Great Hall was always the preferred venue for feasting, but later the Guard Room was pressed into service. At a Consecration Banquet the newly appointed Bishop was permitted to sit at the head of the table with his cap on his head, while everyone else, including the Archbishop, remained with their heads uncovered. I learned this fact from a scholarly book on the subject, but the reason for this quaint custom was not given. I imagine the reason was well known to the Chaplain who, as I have previously indicated, was an authority on headgear.

It was Archbishop Wilberforce who put an end to these jolly occasions in 1845. They were revived later on a much more modest scale and on the evening before the Consecration of a new Bishop, Archbishop Runcie would entertain the cleric and his immediate family to a simple meal and a glass or two of wine. Alas, the custom of wearing a cap at the table had lapsed. Had I possessed the authority, I would certainly have revived it and I suspect I would have received the full support of the Chaplain. It was not a priority for Dr Runcie, however.

This preamble is by way of saying that the Archbishop did his best to be hospitable, but by no means could it be said that the victuals at Lambeth compared in magnificence with the sort of fare provided in Uganda or other parts of the Communion. On his travels the Archbishop was able to sample many exotic dishes and became quite an expert on foods unknown in the Lambeth Road.

Our tale begins when Dr Runcie was sitting at his own table in the small dining room in the Palace. The General Synod had been meeting in Westminster and for day after day had been ploughing through reports produced by clerics labouring in the inner regions of Church House. For much of the week the Archbishop had been required to take the chair and it had taken all his strength to remain awake during the afternoon sessions.

Synod week also saw modest hospitality being offered in the Palace for visiting Bishops from around the country. When the meetings formally closed for the day the Archbishop would wend his weary way back to Lambeth, sign his mail, read his papers for the next day and then do a little entertaining. It was during such an evening that he engaged in conversation with a Bishop who had served for many years in the Far East and was now back in an English diocese.

Bishops of English nationality who had worked overseas and desired to return to their country of birth did not always get charge of a diocese. Some had reached retirement age and came home to put their feet up. Others had retired early in order to make way for a local national and thus had enough energy to continue for another few years. The fortunate ones in this category got a diocese, the less fortunate became assistant bishops, and one or two took on an ordinary parish. The Bishop with whom the Archbishop conversed that evening was an English diocesan who maintained a keen interest in his former territory overseas and in the Far East in general.

'I'm concerned about Burma,' said the cleric as he poked at his shepherd's pie. 'It seems that it's becoming increasingly repressive and I'm afraid that the Church might be in for difficult times.' He had not himself ministered in Burma, but he had worked in a neighbouring country.

The Archbishop listened politely. Every night at the table someone or other was concerned about someone or somewhere. 'I'm concerned about Rupert. I think he might be having domestic troubles.' 'I'm concerned about Mary. Tom might go to Rome at last and leave his wife and children in real difficulties.' The Church was one big hotbed of anxious concern and the Archbishop was the final recipient, on earth at least, of these worries. I assume that the concerned ones also took their problems directly to the Almighty in prayer and thus shared the burden around a bit.

'Really?' said Dr Runcie, welcoming the change from concern about individuals to larger concerns of State. 'I've never been to Burma, you know. Perhaps a tour of the Far East might help somewhat.'

The Bishop assured His Grace that apart from direct divine intervention, nothing else would be so helpful as a full-scale archiepiscopal visitation. There would be difficulties, of course, but it would greatly encourage the locals in their fight for survival. The Archbishop, a past master at the art of survival, warmly responded to this plea and in no time at all the Chaplain and I were busy poring over documents detailing the history of missionary activity in the Far East.

As far as the Anglican Church went, Africa was the jewel in the crown. True, many diligent missionaries had worked long and hard in the exotic countries of the Orient, but – with all respect to them – the results of their labours could not compare at all with African statistics. I think it is fair to say that as a Church we had a much better grasp of African affairs than we ever had of the Far East. After all, what had that fount of

Anglican knowledge, the Revd Sam, told us about where to find rapidly expanding Anglicans? They were certainly not to be found in Thailand.

Apart from research into Church records, some information was needed regarding the current state of political affairs in the countries we were about to visit. A part of my work was to maintain contact with the Foreign Office who, if the mood suited them, provided us with information of varying degrees of usefulness.

Those conversant with the ways of diplomats and their ilk will know that they are just a little on the secretive side when it comes to information. They are polite to a fault, but their training is such that they never disclose anything that has not previously been reported in at least six newspapers. Even then it is better to deny knowledge of the matter if challenged. Following a so-called briefing session, one would discover that one had been given exactly the same information that had previously been distributed to passengers on Swan Hellenic Cruises.

They are, however, always keen to build up their own store of intelligence. In return for anything they could tell me, I disclosed the precise location of the Lambeth Palace kitchens, exactly what the Archbishop had for breakfast that morning and what drinks he had ordered after he had finished his porridge. Such sensitive information ought never to have been disclosed by someone in my position in return for such scant briefings, but life is one endless round of trade-offs, as we all know.

I met with my diplomatic interrogator in the Foreign Office itself. As we walked down the miles of corridor to his

office we were refreshed by a powerful smell of boiling cabbage. 'They're doing something wrong with the kitchens,' he
muttered apologetically. 'It was like this before I went to China
and when I returned three years later nothing had changed. I
confidently expect that it will still smell like this when I go
overseas again next year.' I took careful note of this intelligence,
as he had clearly only disclosed it under extreme duress.

He took a key from his pocket and ushered me into his
shabby office. 'Take a pew,' he said jovially, no doubt trying to
make me feel at home. 'I'll order some coffee.'

I am afraid that I shall have to draw a veil over the conversation that followed. I may have gone too far in disclosing
what I already have. I can say, however, that before I stepped
once again into the aromatic corridor of government it had
been arranged for Dr Runcie and his party to stay with the
British High Commissioner in Burma. This decision gladdened
my heart and was well worth my disclosing further secrets
about Lambeth Palace to this long-suffering agent of the State.

Back in the more palatial and cabbage-free surroundings of Lambeth, I decided on our itinerary. We would fly to
Thailand, where we would change planes for the short trip
into Burma. From there we would go to Korea, and finally we
would touch down for 24 hours in Hong Kong on our way
home.

The briefing papers were now almost assembled. In
Burma most of our time would be spent visiting the capital,
Rangoon. This was the home of Archbishop Gregory, who
had archiepiscopal responsibilities throughout the region. The
Archbishop was a genial character whom we had all met when

he attended the Primates' Meeting or when we dropped in at the secret meetings of the ACC. He belonged to both bodies. He had two notable characteristics: he was a chain smoker and he loved watching television. The former habit he shared with the majority of the population of Asia. As for the latter, I suspect that on the infrequent occasions when he was given permission to leave his country, the television provided him with an opportunity to catch up with what was happening in the world outside. Rangoon was also where the British High Commission was situated and where, out of the goodness of his heart, the High Commissioner had offered hospitality to Dr Runcie and his team.

A week or so before leaving London, we received a message indicating that Dr Runcie would be welcome to visit Burma but he would not be allowed to speak in public. When we asked for further clarification, we were informed that this meant that on no account would he be permitted to preach in the Anglican cathedral in Rangoon. He could take part in the service, but he would not be allowed to address the assembled faithful. This came as a great relief to the Chaplain, who had enough drafting to do to keep him happy for many a year. It also came as a relief to me, as I might hope to benefit instead from the wisdom of a local orator.

We assumed Dr Runcie had gained the reputation of being a dangerous radical from his Falklands address that had so disturbed the British Prime Minister. However, it was the sort of snub that would have sent most dignitaries running round to the nearest stables to jump on the highest horse they could find. Not so Dr Runcie. He saw it as his clear duty to support the Anglicans of Burma and, sermon or no sermon, that was what he intended to do. Accordingly, one fine afternoon, the dutiful John Brown drove us to that location feared by all regular travellers, Heathrow, where we boarded the plane for the Far East.

'It's like entering a time warp,' said the Chaplain as we drove through the main street of Rangoon. It was indeed. It was as though we had been transported back in time to the great days of the British Empire. There was the main hotel, admittedly needing a coat of paint, but untouched since the 1930s at least. There were hardly any foreign visitors in evidence. They were allowed in the country, but only under rigorous supervision.

The High Commissioner's residence was a cosy little retreat near the bustling town centre. He ushered us in, and several retainers who had been in the employ of the British since colonial days dealt speedily with our luggage. We sat in the cool living room and sipped a drink brought to us by a white-jacketed servant of Empire. The High Commissioner was an old Burma hand, having served in the country several times during his career. He had mastered the language and now, having arrived at the top of his particular tree, was in his final years before retiring to an English seaside town.

'Uncle Monty would very much like to meet you during your stay, Your Grace,' he said, as the Archbishop relaxed and sipped a plain soda water.

I expressed surprise. I was unaware that the Archbishop had relatives in Burma, although, given the fact that he came from a seafaring family of sorts, it was feasible.

'No, no,' said His Excellency. 'Uncle Monty is no relative. He's a very old friend of mine and has some connections with Trinity Hall, Cambridge, I believe.'

Trinity Hall had played a significant part in Dr Runcie's life. When he was elected Dean of the College as a comparatively young man, he met a certain Miss Turner, the lovely young daughter of the Professor of Law who was professor of no Christian belief whatsoever. I imagine the rational Professor was more than a little surprised when he discovered that his favoured offspring had accepted the hand of an Anglican cleric. We were told that Uncle Monty, along with many of Professor Turner's old pupils, had risen to giddy heights in the Burmese legal profession. I suspect that many of his customers did not feel so benevolent towards him as we did, as at one time he was Chief Justice in the country.

'I should like to meet him,' said the Archbishop.

The very next day Uncle Monty trundled into the residence. He was an amiable old man, full of stories of the great days of the British Empire. It was clear that he was one of those delightful individuals one occasionally meets in remote corners of the world who are civilized, interesting and straddle the limitations of culture and politics. I could see why he was a particular friend of our High Commissioner.

I cannot imagine how it was that our conversation turned to food. It might have been that we were all hungry, despite the fact that the temperature was sky-high and sausage and mash were far from our thoughts. 'You must have a Burmese breakfast,' said the High Commissioner.

Uncle Monty nodded his wise old head in agreement. 'Quite delicious,' he said. 'Full of flavour and nourishment.'

The Archbishop looked doubtful. He had long experience of native dishes and he had seen that, while they may have done a power of good to the natives, they had caused much distress to the visitors. 'I always take a light breakfast,' he said. 'You know what I mean, Uncle Monty. The sort of thing we got at Tit Hall.' Uncle Monty beamed.

'Well,' said the High Commissioner, 'I'll see that Terry gets one in the morning.'

We all slept well at the residence. His Excellency was fond of opera and before we retired he played us one or two of his favourite arias, accompanied by a glass or two of Scottish harmony. It was a gentle and relaxing evening.

I awoke early the following morning. From my bedroom I could hear the sounds of Rangoon stirring. Street vendors plied their wares; ancient motor cars chugged along the narrow streets. The High Commissioner had already greeted the dawn when I stepped into the living room. 'Good morning, Terry,' he said politely. 'I understand your breakfast is on the way.'

I had understood that my breakfast, like any other breakfast, would be prepared in the High Commissioner's kitchen. I was wrong. Instructions had been given for a typical Burmese breakfast to be gathered from all corners of Rangoon and delivered to the house.

Within a few moments an aged Burmese appeared at the door, carrying a large basket covered with a white cloth. He laid out the contents on the dining table. After so many years I cannot possibly detail all the delicacies that he had collected. I remember the overall sensation, however, and garlic figured prominently. There was garlic porridge with a few hot chillies thrown in. There was garlic this and garlic that. There was more garlic. There was enough garlic to keep a dozen vampires at bay, not only for the duration of our stay in Burma, but for the rest of our mortal lives. It was a blessing that I have no objection to garlic, as the Chaplain and the Archbishop remained fixated on their garlic-free bacon and eggs, leaving me to do my best with the feast set in front of me. I was not sorry to have tried this local fare so thoughtfully provided by my host, but I confess that it was the one and only Burmese breakfast I have ever eaten.

Given the fact that the Archbishop was virtually under house arrest, there is not too much to record about Burma – except, of course, for the great cathedral service. Prior to the service we visited Archbishop Gregory at his residence. He was a comparatively young man and the proud father of twin daughters. Between puffs on his cigarette, he apologized for the fact that His Grace would be obliged to remain silent during the service. Burma was living under considerable restrictions and they were irksome to the Christian community as well as to the population in general, but he assured us that His Grace of Canterbury would be allowed to give the final blessing. He had secured the services of an elderly retired Burmese Archbishop to preach the sermon.

We repaired to the cathedral. The Archbishop and the Chaplain robed and I hovered at the back of the building, looking for a suitable way to escape for a while should the sermon prove to be too tedious. The cathedral was not an exceptional building. There was a small upstairs gallery at the back, which remained empty although the body of the church was pleasantly full. I do not have memories of an inspiring event. We sang a hymn. There were many prayers in English and

Burmese. We sang another hymn, after which the retired Archbishop tottered towards the pulpit to deliver his oration.

I can imagine that he regarded this day as the pinnacle of his career, and why not? As soon as he began to speak, I realized that he was going to take full advantage of the situation. He announced his text and launched forth. Dr Runcie and the Chaplain gave him their undivided attention. At least they appeared to – they had no choice, being in full public view. After 15 minutes or so, the elderly Churchman was beginning to warm up and it was clear he had a long way to go. I edged myself out of my seat at the back of the church and made for the empty gallery. There was a notable absence of comfortable furniture, but there was an old pew which, under the circumstances, looked inviting. I stretched out on it and within a few moments was sound asleep.

I have no idea how long I remained unconscious, but it must have been for at least half an hour. As I gently returned to Burma, I was conscious of a steady droning in my ears. I sat up and looked over the balcony. The dear old man was still in full flight.

'Well,' said the Chaplain some hours later when we had returned to the comfort of our residence. 'I trust that you will never again complain about the quality or length of our employer's sermons. By the way, do you recollect that simple verse: "I slept, and dreamed that life was Beauty; / I woke, and found that life was Duty"?'

I confessed that I did not know the couplet, and I am afraid that I did complain again, but looking back, I accept that my complaints were really quite unjustified.

Having fulfilled our simple duties in Burma, we set sail for Korea. In those days Korea was a special area of responsibility for the Archbishop of Canterbury. Given the somewhat erratic nature of Anglican provincial administration in the Far East, it had not yet been decided if Korea should become a province by itself or if it should join another area. Until such weighty matters could be determined, Korea came under the direct responsibility of the Archbishop of Canterbury. It was a matter of regret for Dr Runcie that, Korea being some considerable distance from Lambeth, he had not been able to pop down for the weekend to see that everything was running smoothly.

Alas, the Church is no different from any other organization when it comes to keeping on the straight and narrow. I hesitate to write truisms, but it is nevertheless a fact that the mice will play when the cat resides a continent away. The Anglican Church in Korea consisted of three dioceses only, and thus there were only three Bishops. Disturbing reports had reached Lambeth Palace that one diocese was not receiving the attention it deserved as its Bishop was frequently absent attending to the management of his family laundry business in San Francisco. As the other two Korean Bishops did not have the proper authority to caution their errant brother, the problem lingered on. The laundry business caused Dr Runcie some amusement, but he clearly recognized that it was a state of affairs which needed cleaning up. He further realized that the sooner Korea could take full and proper responsibility for its own spiritual life the better it would be for everyone.

In accordance with my usual practice, I had made a previous visit to Korea and had discovered that although the laundry and dry-cleaning business appeared to thrive, the education of the clergy was in a precarious state. The finances of the Church were somewhat rocky and there were several other issues that needed dealing with. One pleasurable surprise for me had been to discover what accomplished musicians the Koreans were. The choir in the tiny Anglican cathedral in Seoul was truly excellent, far superior to many church choirs I had listened to in other parts of the world. Good singing would not remedy administrative deficiencies, however, and an archiepiscopal visit was put in motion.

I mentioned at the outset of this chapter that on overseas visits Dr Runcie was favoured with good hospitality and was frequently urged to sample local dishes. Korea was no exception to this rule. Visitors to this exotic part of the world will know that every good Korean loves *kimchi*. This national dish appears to be nothing more than fermented cabbage, similar, I suppose, to the sauerkraut which is so appreciated by the Germans. Every self-respecting Korean will gather cabbages in season and lay them down in stone jars which they keep in a cool place. When the fermentation process is complete the cabbage is ready for the table, and a dish of it seems to appear on every possible occasion. Dr Runcie and his obedient staff sampled *kimchi* and with polite overstatement declared it 'interesting'. Now, many years later, I can say that I thought it was revolting. In case any Korean should stumble across these pages, I ought to say that I have no objection whatsoever if he or she wishes to denigrate fish and chips, Yorkshire pudding or any other delicacy enjoyed by the British. Each to their own.

I have only a hazy memory of the events we attended in Korea. Most of the time was spent attempting to understand what on earth was going on. We were greeted at every turn with smiles and were warmly welcomed, but – as is so often the case in the East – the problems that caused the Korean Church so much grief were never mentioned directly. They were not sorted out for many years, in truth, but I am happy to report that today the Anglican Church in Korea is free from the oversight of Canterbury, and I believe the matter of the laundry was also resolved some years ago.

At the time of our visit, frantic preparations were taking place in Korea for the Olympic Games. A huge stadium was almost completed and Dr Runcie was invited to inspect this building and make approving noises. We were given a briefing beforehand about this magnificent structure. It contained a brand new electronic scoreboard, we were told. This scoreboard was deadly accurate. There could be no dispute. Everything recorded on it would be correct, and everyone would be able to have immediate access to totally accurate information.

Suitably impressed, we drove across the city to the site. There was the customary collection of yellow-painted tractors, scaffolding and men in hard hats, and the building was almost completed. We processed through the main doors into the Temple of Sport and immediately our eyes lifted up towards the illuminated scoreboard.

We found that it displayed a message, and the message was for none other than the distinguished visitor from Canterbury. 'WELCOME,' it proclaimed in letters several feet high. 'WELCOME TO KOREA ARCHBISHOP LUNCHIE.'

As the Chaplain pointed out, one could not fault the sentiments, and it was fitting that the hospitable attributes of our employer had been recognized so many miles away from Lambeth Palace.

16
A Bit of a Squash

Dr Runcie was a hardworking Archbishop conscious of the ancient office he had inherited. Many an evening would see him sitting in his study overlooking the Lambeth gardens and working on his papers long into the night. It was curiously appropriate that he should be sitting in that particular room during the night watch, because before the family apartment was constructed at the top of the Palace, the living quarters were on the first floor and the study he sat in was then a bedroom. That was all in the last century, of course. The Palace has undergone many changes in its long history, but it still retains the atmosphere of a home even though it is also a busy administrative centre for the Church of England.

There was a time when the occupants of Lambeth were deeply involved in matters of State and the Palace was buzzing with politicians from Westminster. Earlier I made reference to the minor skirmishes between Dr Runcie and some Members of Parliament. The problems he experienced were as nothing compared with those his predecessors had to endure. In 1371 it was recorded that the temporal Lords and Commons strongly objected to the fact that so many high offices of State were occupied by clerics. This was due, of course, to the well-known fact that the clergy were educated and could read and write. Note was taken of the protest and for a while laymen were appointed in their place. Alas, this resulted in such a muddle in the country that the learned clerics were quickly called back into service. Out of 16 Archbishops of Canterbury in the fourteenth and fifteenth centuries, 11 were Lord Chancellors. The first Primate to occupy the office of Lord Treasurer was St Dunstan in the tenth century, and the last was Juxton in the seventeenth. There were even two Primates who presided as Chief Justice.

Lambeth Palace has also seen many royal visitors in its time. Edward III came to stay in 1345. Henry VIII called by, and created Charles Somerset, Earl of Worcester (an interesting mingling of counties). Queen Mary frequently visited her favourite, Cardinal Pole, and provided much of his furniture, although there was none in evidence in my day. Queen Elizabeth I also had her favourite, Archbishop Matthew Parker, but as she had difficulty in accepting a married priesthood she kept out of the way of the Archbishop's wife. This was a sensible move, as Archbishop's wives have been known to be somewhat forceful over the years. King Charles I gave away Lady Mary Villiers to James Stuart at Lambeth Palace, and to this day a visitor to the Lambeth library may see, if they are so disposed, a pair of the King's gloves – worn, it is said, as he ascended the scaffold.

There is one dramatic royal story that is certainly worth telling. The night of 9 December 1688 was wet and blustery. To the surprise of the Lambeth gatekeeper, an Italian washer-woman appeared at the Palace entrance carrying what seemed to be a bundle of washing under her arm. The supposed wash-erwoman turned out to be none other than Mary of Modena, the unfortunate wife of James II (who was supplanted by William of Orange), and the 'washing' was a bundle containing the six-month-old Prince of Wales, later to be known as 'The Pretender'. Mary was heading for the coast on the very night that the King himself had fled, and she had crossed by boat from Horseferry Road to land at the Lambeth stairs. Alas, trans-port in those days was as unreliable as it is today, and she found that the Gravesend coach was nowhere to be seen. She shel-tered by Morton's Gateway until the coach finally arrived and spirited her away.

As the Archbishop sat in his study during the long night hours, he might also remember the days when the Palace was very nearly destroyed. Wat Tyler's mob, who murdered Archbishop Sudbury at Tower Hill, set fire to the Palace in 1381. Some 500 demonstrators threatened Archbishop Laud 200 years later, but were turned away at the last moment before they could cause any damage. The speedy arrival of troops during the Gordon Riots in 1780 enabled Archbishop

Cornwallis and his family to flee across the river, and once again the Palace escaped destruction. Finally, in World War II, a German bomb found its mark and caused considerable devastation. To this day the repair work for the damage done by the bomb can still be seen.

Running like a thread through the history of Lambeth and its occupants was the age-old struggle by the Papacy to dominate the monarch of England. This was matched by the determination of the Bishops to retain their links with Rome and yet at the same time to maintain their independence. This was a political game repeated across the centuries. No less than six Archbishops received the red hat of a Cardinal. In fact there were seven, but Robert Kilwardby is not usually included in the list because when he was made Cardinal Bishop of Portus and Sancta Rufina in 1278 he was forced to resign the See of Canterbury. Unfortunately, he took with him many records which have not seen the light of day since. Following the Reformation, of course, there have been no Cardinal Archbishops of Canterbury.

I have really mentioned all the above simply to illustrate that behind each and every occupant of the See of Canterbury there lies an enormous weight of history. It is not only the history of England and the British Isles, but also a part of the history of the universal Church.

It was often necessary for Dr Runcie to work on his papers late at night because, when he was not out and about in the world, there was a steady stream of visitors to Lambeth during the hours of daylight. Not all were able to see him in person, even though the vast majority wanted to. Some would be entertained by the Bishop at Lambeth, a senior Bishop responsible for seeing that the Lambeth administration functioned as well as anything in the Church of England, which is not saying much. The Chaplain would also take on his fair share of supplicants and many of those from overseas would find their way to my door.

The annual Lambeth garden party for missionaries was the one event of the year when my secretary was kept more than busy. Invitations were sent out to missionary societies, missionaries on furlough (home leave) and retired missionaries. It fell to me to ensure that this occasion went like clockwork and that every missionary shook the hand of the Archbishop and his wife before getting a cup of tea and a bun. It was none too easy to organize.

The staff at Buckingham Palace, who have the misfortune to arrange several garden parties each summer, solve the problem of individuals being greeted by the monarch in a very simple manner. They preselect a small group and put them in a special enclosure where the Queen can easily manage to exchange a word or two with a few dozen people. The remainder might get a royal wave if they are lucky. At the Lambeth missionary event the group was not large enough to separate out a few from the flock, but it was too large for the Archbishop to spend more than a few seconds with each individual. Consequently a long queue would form across the front courtyard while Dr and Mrs Runcie attempted to say something meaningful to ecclesiastical warriors from Africa, Asia and other far-flung parts of the Communion. The Revd Sam was drafted in to help on these occasions, but there was not much that he could do. Each individual wanted to shake hands with their host and tell something, if not all, of their life story.

After my first experience of the garden party, I decided that the missionaries ought to be entertained in the front courtyard whilst lining up to enter the Palace and shake the hand of the Archbishop. Once again the Services came to our aid, this time in the shape of the band of the Grenadier Guards. Although the courtyard was quite spacious enough for the band to march up and down, that clearly would have interfered with the orderly queuing system and so it was decided that they should be seated by the front door, just across from an ancient fig tree.

This tree, incidentally, is quite a marvel. It is said that Cardinal Pole planted two very large fig trees in the old garden at Lambeth. Sadly they died or were destroyed in the alterations that were made to the Palace in 1829. All was not lost, however. Some diligent gardener managed to secure an off-shoot and planted it just by the wall of the Great Hall. There (unlike the Cardinal's royal furniture) it remains to this day.

Preparations continued apace for the great missionary day. The services of a worthy missionary Bishop were secured to preach a sermon in the chapel; the Revd Sam assured us he would be on hand to engage in diplomatic activities; an army of helpers was briefed to pour tea and serve cakes. Finally, short biographical details of all the participants were prepared so that the Archbishop would be able to greet each visitor like a long-lost cousin.

'Well,' said the Chaplain as we chatted in his room a day or so before the event, 'another missionary festival looms. You won't require me, I'm sure. I really must get across to the British Library that afternoon.' To be fair to the Chaplain, he certainly bore no animosity towards missionaries, but he did have to endure more than his share of large gatherings and if he could be spared from time to time he was grateful.

'Oh, by the way,' he said, as I was about to leave, 'you do know that Princess Margaret is coming to lunch that day, don't you?'

I stopped in the doorway. 'That's pushing it a bit,' I replied. 'The missionaries start to line up soon after one o'clock, and the gates are opened at two.'

'I don't know what's happened,' said the Chaplain. 'Some confusion about dates. It's a very small luncheon and shouldn't last too long.'

As Princess Margaret had never been known to protest against married Archbishops I assumed that, as well as the Archbishop, Mrs Runcie would also be present. Neither of them might be free to shake the missionaries' hands at the appointed hour. If by any chance the luncheon party lingered over coffee, then the worthy Grenadiers might have to be deployed at the gates on military duties of a more aggressive nature. Not only that, but one also had to take into account the fact that the Archbishop became a trifle anxious when receiving visitors. It was not only royal visitors who caused him anxiety, but visitors of any description. He needed to be assured that every detail had been taken care of so that their visit might be smooth and enjoyable. It promised to be an interesting afternoon.

Finally the great day dawned. Although Lambeth Palace is a fair-sized building, it had to manage with a rather limited domestic staff. On days such as the missionaries' garden party the staff were stretched to their limits. Given the added pressure of a royal luncheon party, they were in fact pushed right against the wall. Mrs Skinner, a gentle and charming domestic helper, had been at Lambeth since the days of Archbishop Michael Ramsey and was quite the most unflappable of individuals. She attended to the luncheon party, which was set up in the State Room situated next to the Archbishop's study. This attractive room overlooked the gardens and in 1829 had been designated the State Drawing Room. Now it was used for official events, although signs of domesticity were evident. On the grand piano there was a notice which read, 'Do not place anything on Mrs Runcie's piano.' Such a notice might seem somewhat abrupt, but long experience of public gatherings had shown that respect for polished furniture is low on the public agenda. Perhaps the good Cardinal had similar problems and secured his precious royal armchairs behind the Vatican walls.

Out in the garden anxious eyes were cast heavenwards in an attempt to determine the weather. The forecast that morning had not been good and showers were threatened for the afternoon. During the morning men from the royal protection squad roamed through the Palace looking for suspect packages. Shortly before one o'clock, a royal limousine purred through the gates. A small band of missionaries had already gathered and they raised a surprised cheer for the royal personage reclining in the back seat. Soon afterwards the missionaries' early arrival was to be rewarded yet again when a coach was admitted containing the band of the Grenadier Guards, together with their instruments. The gatekeeper assured the missionaries that they would be admitted soon after two o'clock, as indicated on their invitation cards.

Back in the Palace, Mrs Skinner served lunch in the semidomestic serenity of the State Room. The Princess was in relaxed mood and settled down to a cordial afternoon with the Archbishop and his wife. More missionaries gathered outside the main gate. At a few minutes before two o'clock, the gate-keeper asked for permission to open the gates to allow the patient missionaries to form an orderly queue in the courtyard whilst waiting to be received by the Archbishop. The royal security men who had been lurking in every corner shook their heads. No one could be admitted until the Princess had left.

By now the queue awaiting admission had grown considerably. The band had decked themselves out in their best uniforms and stood ready to play pleasing melodies from their repertoire. It began to rain. The Grenadiers scurried for shelter. Outside the walls, missionaries accustomed to facing every form of hazard this planet can devise produced umbrellas and waited stoically. In the State Room Mrs Skinner served pudding. The rain stopped and the Grenadiers remustered. Mrs Skinner served coffee. The missionaries waited. The rain started again. At about three-thirty the royal guest, totally unaware of the impending garden party, rose to leave and was both surprised and delighted to receive such a rousing cheer as she departed through the gates. The patient missionaries trooped across the courtyard to the gentle strains of Gilbert and Sullivan and were warmly received by their hosts.

That evening, when all was peaceful, I sat with Dr Runcie in his study. He had put his papers to one side for a moment and was warming himself by the artificial coal fire. 'It was all a bit of a squash,' he said, as he mused on the packed afternoon, 'but they all enjoyed it and so did I. Thank goodness for the Scots Guards. They saved the day.'

I remain convinced that it was the Grenadiers, but the Archbishop will have none of it. The matter remains one of friendly disagreement between the two of us.

17
All at Sea

Many years ago, it was disputes at Canterbury that caused Archbishop Baldwin to seek more peaceful pastures at Lambeth Palace on the bank of the Thames. The site of the Archbishops' London home predated Baldwin, however, for it is believed that he built on the remains of a medieval manor house and even before that there may have been a Roman settlement there.

Long before Lambeth Bridge was built, this part of the Thames was a popular and busy crossing point. Before the embankments were constructed, the gardens of the Palace extended down to the river and many Prelates kept a barge moored there so that they might sail gently to St Paul's, or other suitable locations in the city. At the time of the wedding of Prince Charles and Lady Diana Spencer I attempted to persuade Dr Runcie to resurrect this ancient custom and sail to the cathedral in a naval barge. Wisely he said that he would have none of it, as he believed that such a voyage might be interpreted as an attempt to upstage the royal couple. It was left to John Brown to pilot the stretched Granada through the crowded streets of the city to the steps of St Paul's for the royal wedding.

Once inside the cathedral, the Archbishop donned his cope and mitre, specially hand-embroidered for the occasion, and the following day, true to form, certain members of the fourth estate accused the poor man of attempting to compete with the bride for sartorial magnificence. He might as well have gone the whole hog and enjoyed a pleasant sail down the Thames after all.

Throughout his time at Lambeth, Archbishop Runcie never commissioned a new archiepiscopal barge and, as far as I am aware, his successor has not done so either. Perhaps on the day when all private vehicles are barred from the city streets this ancient custom might be revived at last. I live in hope.

Some time later we did get an opportunity to sail with the Royal Navy in HMS *Invincible*. Not, of course, to St Paul's Cathedral, but while the ship was engaged in exercises off Portland.

I have mentioned earlier that the Archbishop had served his country with distinction in the Scots Guards. Like most ex-members of the Household Brigade, he took a keen interest in the doings of his old regiment. On one occasion when we were entertained to dinner by the Guards, a piper appeared and marched around the table playing a melody specially composed for the event entitled 'Dr Robert Runcie, MC'. To my untrained ear (untrained to Scottish music, that is), it sounded like any other lament, but we were assured that it was unique. The title, of course, left some room for confusion. 'In years to come,' quipped the Archbishop when we were travelling home, 'someone will ask, "Who was that Scottish MO named Runcie?"'

Dr Runcie was quite understandably fond of his old regiment, but as Archbishop of Canterbury he had to display that impartiality which comes so unnaturally to most of us. He could not be seen to be partial to any one branch of the Services and so, from time to time, he would travel to visit the Royal Air Force or the Navy. The visit to *Invincible* was designed to enable the Archbishop to see something of life on the high seas and also to get to know one or two of the naval Chaplains.

It was a blustery morning when we walked together down the long staircase at Lambeth. John Brown, formally dressed in a smart grey uniform with cap to match, was on hand to greet us and within moments we were passing through the main gates of the Palace and out into the busy London streets, bound for Portland.

We did not embark immediately on arrival, but spent the day visiting the various shore establishments that clutter this part of the English coast. I have never been particularly fond of such places and the passing of the years has totally obliterated that day from my memory. I have a vague recollection of attending a reception and dinner at the military home of an Admiral and I believe we may have stayed the night there. I do remember that the next day we travelled to *Invincible* by naval helicopter.

In those days, and I have no reason to believe that matters are any different today, military helicopters were excessively noisy. The only form of soundproofing was a gigantic pair of headphones, which simply increased the general noise level by adding incomprehensible military chatter to the general background din of the rotors. There was a considerable volume of chatter between our pilot and his command post as we prepared to take off. We soon realized that, in between receiving commands, he was also issuing instructions to us, as every so often he would turn round and gesture in our general direction. We nodded wisely and as we eventually arrived on board *Invincible* safely, we can only assume that we followed our instructions to the letter.

I was very much looking forward to visiting *Invincible* because, at the age of 15, I had informed my father that I wanted to finish my studies and join the Royal Navy. To cut a long story short, my father talked me out of it and I was spared from spending most of my teenage years at that notorious shore-training establishment, HMS *Ganges*. As a boy I fondly imagined that sailors would spend much of their time enjoying gentle sea breezes and visiting exotic locations, where they would feast on pineapples and fresh fish and enjoy the company of local beauties. How wrong can one be?

Sadly, my illusions were finally shattered when the aircraft carrier *Invincible* proved to be an even greater nightmare than the familiar and dreaded Heathrow. We clambered from the helicopter and battled against the wind to greet a welcoming party who had lined up to receive the Archbishop. Despite what seemed to be a force nine gale, the air was thick with the smell of aviation fuel.

We were quickly ushered below where, it seemed, the vast majority of the crew spent most of their lives. Unless they happened to be one of the very few charged with flagging aircraft on and off the carrier, or one of the even fewer manning the bridge, they might just as well have been in a hangar at Heathrow. 'So much is under cover,' said our helpful guide, 'in case of nuclear fall-out. We need to be able to protect as many of the crew as possible.'

We were taken through an enormous hangar where aircraft, their wings folded like grotesque sleeping insects, waited to be hauled on deck and catapulted into the blue. Back on deck, we watched with admiration as a pilot brought his fighter plane down to make a perfect landing on the heaving deck, where he was snatched to a halt by a menacing-looking hook and stowed away in a matter of minutes. 'We have to be quick,' our guide shouted. 'In conditions of war we can't afford to have fighters waiting for hours to land.' As he spoke, another plane zoomed in and was promptly manhandled away by the valiant deck crew.

We went below again to find our quarters. Out of courtesy the Archbishop had been given the finest berth on the ship, the space reserved for the Admiral. In all fairness I have to say that although it was spacious (compared to the other quarters we saw), the meanest, cheapest room in a downtown drive-in motel would look like a suite in The Savoy by comparison. 'First and foremost this is a fighting machine,' our host reiterated. 'There's not much room for luxury on board.' I thought of sea breezes and pineapples and silently thanked my father for his wisdom, which had been so ill-received so many years previously.

When we had unpacked our tour continued. We entered a gloomy cavern where sailors spent the whole of their time watching flickering radar screens. We visited the cookhouse where goodness knows how many loaves of bread were baked each day. We saw the lower ranks' quarters and I immediately determined that only direct entry into the Service with at least the rank of Admiral could possibly have suited me. For such a huge ship, it was all very cramped, very clean, very military.

'Is there any particular part of the ship you would like to visit, Archbishop?' asked our indefatigable guide. Lord Runcie, more accustomed to being confined in a tank of the Guards Armoured Brigade, hesitated.

I stepped in. 'What about the Chinese shoemaker?' I suggested. Dr Runcie looked puzzled.

'Are you sure?' responded our escort. 'It's rather a long way to walk.'

I assured him that that was where we wanted to go and, when Dr Runcie nodded his head, off we went. As we processed, heads bowed because of the limited headroom, I explained to Dr Runcie who it was we were going to visit. I had learned that it had long been a tradition in the Navy that on some of the larger ships a couple of Hong Kong Chinese were given space somewhere in the remoter depths of the vessel.

There, in the bowels of the ship, they toiled day and night to produce hand-made leather shoes, silk shirts and fine suits for members of the crew. These products were for civilian use, of course, and the craftsmen charged what they considered to be a fair commercial price for the goods.

'I suspect this is the first time an Archbishop has paid such a visit,' said our pilot as he steered us past huge tins of white paint and coils of rope. 'We're nearly there,' he shouted after 20 minutes or so. 'We're almost at the prow.'

We approached a dimly lit den and, as we peered through the gloom, we could just make out a human form tapping away with a small hammer like a character from an ancient French novel. We were assured that his command of English was quite adequate, but he rarely spoke it. All we would have to do would be to let him know our requirements and in no time at all they would be ready. Dr Runcie and I conferred together and decided that we could both make excellent use of a pair of hand-made leather shoes.

Quick as a flash, the shoemaker/tailor put down his hammer and produced a ledger of the sort that was in use when Dickens was a lad. He gestured to the Archbishop to remove his shoe and then signalled him to place his purple sock in the centre of the page. He took a pencil and carefully drew around the left foot and then the right, leaving a perfect image in the book. He then produced a tape measure and when the necessary measurements had been taken he presented the Archbishop with an advertisement torn out of a magazine. It portrayed several styles of shoe. The Archbishop selected a black Oxford brogue and I followed his good example. That was that. Several weeks later a parcel arrived at Lambeth Palace from the Chaplain on the *Invincible* containing two pairs of leather shoes. They were excellent.

There is a sequel to this little tale. At regular intervals following our visit to the Navy, we sent further orders for shoes via the Chaplain and were always completely satisfied. Then we heard some terrible news. It had been decided by the Ministry of Defence that HMS *Invincible* was no longer needed and could be safely sold off to Australia. We were thrown into despair and had visions of our very own personal shoemaker sailing away with his precious ledger to make a whole new collection of footwear for our Australian cousins. As so often happens, however, fate intervened. The Falklands War broke out and the Royal Navy retained our shoemaker, along with HMS *Invincible*.

Only last week I went with Lord Runcie, now long retired, to watch the cricket in Canterbury. I glanced at his footwear. Sure enough, he was wearing his Chinese Oxford brogues, just as I was wearing mine. We do indeed have a great deal for which to thank the Royal Navy.

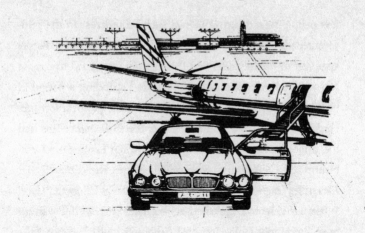

18

Dr Runcie, I presume?

In 1629 Bishop Laud, then Bishop of London and later to become Archbishop of Canterbury, had occasion to issue a stiff reprimand. It was directed at a certain Dr Alexander Leighton. The Bishop, together with his colleagues in the Star Chamber, took exception to a book written by Dr Leighton. Their annoyance was understandable, since the book was entitled *Zion's Plea against the Prelacy*. The doctor was not a man to mince his words. Within the pages of his treatise he 'counselled the killing of all the Bishops' and called the Queen 'a Canaanite and an idolatress'.

Today, when biblical knowledge is not what it was and respect for Bishops and the monarchy has declined somewhat, few people would turn a hair at such sentiments. In the mid-seventeenth century, however, such intemperate language hardly appealed to the Royalists and Dr Leighton was called to pay for his sins by having his ears cropped and spending a period of time in the stocks. As we all know too well, political fortunes change like the wind and as soon as the Parliamentarians had the upper hand, and on the very day when Laud, now Archbishop of Canterbury, was called before the Council, Dr Alexander Leighton was appointed head jailer at Lambeth Palace. When Dr Leighton appeared at the main gate with a warrant from the Honourable House of Commons and demanded the keys, all poor Archbishop Laud could say was, 'I refer myself to God.'

During this politically turbulent period in English history, many large country houses were commandeered by Parliament. When the 'common jails', as they were called, were filled with the principal clergy and gentry of the kingdom, the 'venerable old houses where so many excellent and pious Bishops had for a long course of years lived in splendour and hospitality' were requisitioned and converted into prisons. Lambeth Palace was seized and the installation of Dr Leighton as jailer saw the end of what little 'splendour and hospitality' Archbishop Laud had enjoyed. He died on the scaffold at Tower Hill on 10 January 1645.

As might be expected, Alexander Leighton, a native of Scotland, did not endear himself to his charges. Those who had little love for the Scots said that he 'persecuted their purses with as much rigour and severity as he did their persons'. The exact date of Leighton's death is not known, but it is said that he died 'out of his mind' in 1644, although some claim to have seen him alive the following year.

There are records of some prisoners escaping from Lambeth. One, Dr Guy Carleton, was fortunate enough to have a devoted and ingenious wife, who somehow managed to smuggle a rope into the Water Tower where her husband was languishing. Unfortunately the rope was too short. Having descended its length, the agile Dr Guy let go, only to fracture and dislocate his legs. Painfully he dragged himself to the river and was hauled into a small boat, in which he made good his escape to France. Several years later he received his earthly reward when he was appointed Bishop of Bristol and later Bishop of Chichester.

All the above events – and more – came to mind when, over 300 years later, I found myself idling the days away in a very different prison in the Middle East. Although I had no doubts about the devotion of my own wife, given the fact that I was secured in a secret location many miles from home, and heavy metal shutters covered the windows of my cell, there was little prospect of emulating the exploits of Dr Guy.

Sitting alone, I frequently cast my mind back to the days spent at Lambeth Palace. In my mind I walked through the ancient building, remembering what I could of the many Archbishops who had lived there before Dr Runcie. Most, if not all, had in some way or another been drawn into the politics of their day, some gladly, others more reluctantly. Although Archbishop Runcie might fairly be described as an old-fashioned liberal, there was no way in which he could legitimately be accused of undue political interference. His involvement, and the involvement of his staff, in working for the release of hostages in Iran, Libya and Lebanon was prompt-ed and motivated by humanitarian concerns.

In political terms, my return to the Middle East at a time of heightened duplicity and acute risk was virtually suicidal, but the decision to return was not taken principally on politi-cal grounds. Our motives were humanitarian and the decision to go back was taken from that basis. In fairness, I must say that it was with some degree of reluctance that Dr Runcie agreed to my returning and when eventually I was captured and had time for prolonged reflection, I felt sympathy for the Archbishop. I knew that he would feel personally responsible for the situation even though, had he not allowed me to return as a member of his staff, I would have resigned and returned to Lebanon independently.

For several years I was kept in strict solitary confinement and received no news whatsoever of the world outside my cell. I often wondered how Richard was faring in his new role as the incumbent of a busy London parish, how John had coped with the visit we had planned to Japan, and who had taken my place on the team. Then, one day, my total solitude was broken. After tapping on the wall of my cell for years on end, I received an answering tap. It came from the hostage next door, Terry Anderson, and he had a radio. When he had given me what news he had of my family, I enquired about Lambeth and the Archbishop. Had he any information? As Terry was American, and a Roman Catholic to boot, his knowledge of (and interest in) the doings of the Archbishop of Canterbury was limited to say the least. He thought there had been some mention recent-ly, but he could not be sure. He promised to listen carefully.

Some weeks later he tapped out the news. Dr Runcie had retired and a new Archbishop had been appointed.

The years passed slowly and eventually I – together with other Western hostages – was released. After a short journey in the boot of a car, I was transferred to the front seat of another vehicle and eventually landed up at the residence of the British Ambassador to Syria. It was here, in this ancient biblical city of Damascus, that I was reunited with my old friend and former travelling companion, the Chaplain. Richard Chartres was one of the group who had flown out to the Middle East to collect me.

Although he was not given to demonstrative gestures, on this occasion he made an exception, smiled and held out his hand. For once in his life he was without a notebook. I shuffled onto the plane in my ill-fitting, second-hand clothes and we sat together. I remembered our first meeting years ago in St Albans. Much had happened since then.

'It's really good of you to be here,' I said, rather at a loss for words after so many years of silence. As we flew towards England I remembered the numerous times we had travelled together, briefing the Archbishop *en route* to our destination. Now Richard was briefing me. He told me that Dr Runcie was well and would be at the airport when we arrived.

Several hours passed and eventually we entered British airspace. A traditional welcome had been laid on for me, consisting of gale-force winds and driving rain. The enthusiasm of the elements was such that it was rumoured that a landing at the designated airport might not be possible and we might have to be diverted. I remembered downtown Burbank and other disaster areas. I was beginning to feel quite at home already.

The cabin crew made their final tour of inspection, complete with large plastic sacks into which they deposited the familiar rubbish that inevitably accumulates during a lengthy flight. As they wanted everything to appear in good order when the Archbishop and other VIPs came on board, they crammed these sacks into the only space available: the small toilet situated next to the door at the front of the plane.

Like many rumours, those circulating on the aeroplane proved to be groundless. The skilful Captain bumped his craft through the turbulence, landed at the correct airport and taxied towards a hangar.

'Wait here,' said Richard with his customary authority. 'Dr Runcie will come on first and have a few words privately. Then everyone else will board.' He disappeared to locate the welcoming party.

I waited patiently. Through the window I could see crowds of photographers gathered in the distance. I continued to wait. Richard returned.

'There's been a delay,' he explained. 'Nothing to worry about. Dr Runcie doesn't seem to have arrived yet, but he'll be along in a moment.' He disappeared again.

I thought of the times I had uttered similar soothing words to the Archbishop when everything was going haywire and I simply did not have a clue what was happening. Richard returned yet again.

'It's been decided that the Foreign Secretary and others will come on board and have a few words now,' he told me. 'Dr Runcie doesn't seem to be here yet, but we're assured he's on his way.'

Several cheerful individuals appeared in the cabin and dripped gently towards me. As I was engaging in a little polite conversation, suddenly there was a squeal of brakes and a saloon car pulled up at the foot of the aircraft steps. Out leapt the familiar figure of Dr Runcie. Without pausing for breath, he took the steps two at a time, turned left instead of right and wrenched open the toilet door, only to disappear beneath a mountain of plastic refuse. Richard temporarily resumed his former duties as Chaplain and hastily retrieved the situation by guiding his charge safely down the aisle in my direction.

'Dr Runcie, I presume?' I said somewhat unimaginatively.

The former Archbishop gave me a broad smile. Richard took a step back and scribbled a note on a small piece of paper. It was just like old times.

Index